General editor: Graham Hand

Brodie's Notes on D. H. Lawrence's

Women in Love

Graham Handley MA PhD
Formerly Principal Lecturer in English, All Saints College, Tottenham

Pan Books London, Sydney and Auckland

First published 1989 by Pan Books Ltd,
Cavaye Place, London SW10 9PG
9 8 7 6 5 4 3 2 1

ISBN 0 330 50279 4
Photoset by Parker Typesetting Service, Leicester
Printed and bound in Great Britain by
Richard Clay Ltd, Bungay, Suffolk

Contents

Page references are to the Penguin edition of *Women in Love* but as references are also given to particular chapters, the Notes may be used with any edition of the book.

Preface

The intention throughout this study aid is to stimulate and guide, to encourage the reader's *involvement* in the text, to develop disciplined critical responses and a sure understanding of the main details in the chosen text.

Brodie's Notes provide commentaries on chapters, scenes or individual poems as appropriate. These are designed to underline the most important literary and factual details. Textual notes will accompany these commentaries: these will be explanatory or critical (sometimes both), defining what is difficult or obscure on the one hand, or stressing points of character, style, plot or an aspect of critical evaluation on the other. Revision questions will be set on each act or group of chapters or poems in order to test the student's careful application to the text of the prescribed book.

The second section of each of these study aids will consist of a critical examination of the author's art. This will cover such major elements as characterization, style, structure, setting, theme(s) or any other aspect of the book which the editor considers needs close study. The paramount aim is to send the reader back to the text. Each study aid will include a series of general questions which require a detailed knowledge of the set book; the first of these questions will have notes by the editor of what *might* be included in a written answer. A short list of books considered useful as background reading for the student will be provided at the end.

Graham Handley

The author and his work

David Herbert Lawrence was born at Eastwood, Nottinghamshire, in 1885. He was the youngest in a family of four, his father being a miner who had worked in the pits from the age of seven. His mother, immortalized as Mrs Morel in *Sons and Lovers*, came from a middle-class family. The boy's health was suspect from the beginning, and he was certainly not strong enough to become a collier. At the age of thirteen he won a scholarship to Nottingham High School, and later, for a short period, took a job as a clerk. He left his post in order to train as a teacher and, after two years at Nottingham University College, he emerged very highly placed indeed. He taught in Croydon – some of his poems and many of his letters record the experience – and it was while he was there that his first novel, *The White Peacock* (1911), was published.

By now Lawrence was writing poems and stories regularly, seeing his future as that of a professional writer. His mother, to whom he was devoted, died in 1910, and some eighteen months after her death he met and fell in love with Frieda Weekley. She was a member of the distinguished German von Richthoften family. At the time she was married to Ernest Weekley, a professor at Nottingham University College. In 1912 she and Lawrence went to Germany together and in 1914, after her divorce from Weekley, they were married.

They were in England during the war years, staying for a time in a cottage in Cornwall, where Frieda was suspected of being a spy. Lawrence, who loathed the Germans and the Allies about equally, was physically unfit for military service. After the war the Lawrences left England and travelled extensively, first in Europe, where they visited Frieda's family, and then in Australia and America. A considerable period of their life together was spent in New Mexico on a ranch which had been given to them by a sympathizer. Throughout these years of travel and temporary settlement, Lawrence was a prolific writer of poems, stories and novels; he wrote about whatever caught his interest – literary evaluations and sometimes eccentric critical commentaries, books on travel and history. His letters are a mine of information about the man, and they are written with a characteristic independence, forthrightness, and, it must be allowed, bloody-mindedness too. He and Frieda returned to Europe in 1929. For some time the condition of his lungs had given cause for concern, and he finally died of tuberculosis in Vence, near Nice, on 2 March 1930.

In an excellent essay on Lawrence (*The Pelican Guide to English Literature, 7, The Modern Age*, pp.280–300), W. W. Robson, before analysing *Women in Love*, highlights the difficulties in giving a balanced view of D. H. Lawrence. It is sufficient here to say that the skeletal career drawn above had its life in the flesh and blood of unique inspiration. But when that is said, one is faced with a mass of literature – anecdotal, critical, defamatory, laudatory – beneath which the real D. H. Lawrence, man and artist, lies buried.

Shortly after his death Catherine Carswell published *The Savage Pilgrimage* (1932), a sympathetic account of Lawrence's life as she knew it, based on her friendship with him. In the previous year the critic John Middleton Murry published his account, largely unsympathetic, in *Son of Woman, The Story of D. H. Lawrence*. Murry's book derives mainly from the period spent in Cornwall, during which he, the gifted short-story writer Katherine Mansfield and the Lawrences had lived together. Lawrence himself has said that the characters in *Women in Love* are based on the quartet, but 'based' is perhaps too definitive a term. Lawrence always put his friends – and more often his enemies – into his books, and Middleton Murry also has the dubious distinction of figuring in 'Jimmy and the Desperate Woman'. But what we must add is that although Lawrence took from life he wrote mystically and passionately about the spirit with instinct and imagination. If Miriam in *Sons and Lovers* is the Jessie Chambers of Lawrence's young manhood, she is also the fictionalized character who fits the context of that searing novel.

In Lawrence's lifetime he was the centre of controversy, not a little of it arising from his own obstinate attitudes, but most of it unjustified and stemming from the bias of society and the hounding of the self-righteously indignant who sought to crucify the man and his art. *The Rainbow* (1915) was banned for obscenity, as was *Lady Chatterley's Lover* (1928). It was not until the unexpurgated text of the latter was rescued from oblivion and exposed to the glare of notoriety attendant upon a court case (1960) that Lawrence's name was freed from the stigma which he suffered whilst alive.

I do not intend here to look closely at any of Lawrence's individual works, but try to indicate the general nature of his achievement and motivation. If you, as reader, look at novels as different in inception and execution as *The Plumed Serpent* and *Lady Chatterley's Lover*, you will be aware at once that this is no ordinary, conventional novelist operating in the mainstream of the traditional English novel. Lawrence's writing is like no one else's yet, arguably, *Women in Love* is a novel of provincial life, and has certain affinities in form and in spirit of place which characterized great nineteenth-century novels like, say, *The Return of the Native* and *Middlemarch*. The differences, however, are much greater than the similarities. Perhaps the key to these differences lies in what Lawrence wrote to Ernest Collings in the same year (1913) that *Sons and Lovers* was published. In this letter he speaks of his religion as being a belief in the blood and flesh as distinct from the intellect, stressing that we can err in our minds, but that the way our blood reacts, what it tells us to do and believe, is the truth. Lawrence has little time for the mere acquisition of knowledge as such – witness the discussion between Birkin and Hermione in which he accuses her of watching herself, of having it all in the head – and refers to the intellect as a 'bit and bridle'. He sees man's body as 'a kind of flame, like a candle, always upright, always flowing', and the intellect as the light that is shed on things around. Lawrence is not concerned with the things around, but 'with the mystery of the flame forever flowing'.

This mystery was to be explored again and again. What it meant in practice was that Lawrence brought to his novels and stories a new, vivid awareness of the primary things in life. A simple example will indicate the difference between Lawrence and one of his great predecessors, George Eliot, a writer who he admired. When, in *Adam Bede*, the hero confronts the young squire Arthur Donnithorne, seducer of Adam's intended bride, Hetty Sorrel, and fells him with a blow which is delivered finally more in sorrow than in anger, we know nothing of Adam's deepest state of emotion. But when Baxter Dawes and Paul Morel fight in *Sons and Lovers*, or when Hermione thunders the paperweight against Birkin's head, or when Birkin and Gerald struggle, the primitive impulses of the subconscious are revealed. They act without recourse to convention, education, upbringing, and the result is that we touch dimensions of human experience unplumbed before.

Since Lawrence deals with the subconscious, the instinct, it is not surprising that much of his fiction is intimately concerned with one of the primary impulses in man, the sexual drive. From first to last in Lawrence's writing sexual awareness is pre-eminent; in elevating this driving force, and giving to its consummation something of the sublime, Lawrence not only wrote from his heart – and his instinct – but gave to the generations of writers who succeeded him a freedom which has, alas, been widely abused. Those who pointed the finger of accusation at *Lady Chatterley's Lover* must have forgotten the sexuality of, for example, *Hamlet*; they cannot have read with any degree of closeness Chaucer, Fielding, Balzac or Maupassant. Yet even where Lawrence feels most strongly, he is at times contradictory. Paul and Clara fall from the pinnacle of sexual consummation in *Sons and Lovers*, and the same happens to Ursula and Skrebensky in *The Rainbow*. It is not stated overtly, but one has the impression that sexual fulfilment cannot be sustained without an accompanying spiritual fulfilment. In *The Rainbow* it seems that the woman must not submit, but must retain her individuality, her essential being; in *The Plumed Serpent* the woman's physical fulfilment is dependent upon her acceptance of the guiding authority of the man. And, as you will see in *Women in Love*, Gerald's wanting Gudrun wastes her (her words) so much that she has to escape from him. In doing so she knows that she has destroyed him, and she knows that Birkin knows this too. None the less, some of the most beautiful lyrical passages in Lawrence's writings exalt the sexual act without any of the overtones or innuendo which denigrate it in so much of our contemporary fiction and drama.

Lawrence's poetry is of a very high order. His treatment of Nature has been likened to that of Swinburne, who also uncovered some of our deepest sexual impulses. But Swinburne never once saw nature as Lawrence knew her. In the novels and stories there is frequently a symbolic or mystical association with natural description. Consider, for instance, Mrs Morel's experience with the lilies when she is shut out by her drunken husband in *Sons and Lovers*, or the reiterative mention of the flowers in *Odour of Chrysanthemums*, the flowers representing the promise in marriage, and in death the life-in-death which that marriage becomes. Lawrence's prose is imbued with the spirit and practice of his poetry. He was adept at picking up intensely vivid impressions and storing them for use in his writing later.

Another of his major techniques, very common in *Women in Love*,. is the constant emphasis of a sound, a colour, an impression, by the use of multiple repetition. The effect is never diminished, always enhanced and, as in his poetry, there is often a rhythmic quality which registers in the consciouness of the reader. Another aspect of Lawrence's work which must be mentioned in any consideration of his achievement is his mastery of that underrated form, the short story. Some of Lawrence's stories are in fact long, like *The Man Who Died* and *St Mawr*. Some are genuinely short stories, like *Odour of Chrysanthemums* and *The Prussian Officer*. In all his novels it will be noticed that some of the episodes are virtually complete stories in themselves: in *Women in Love* one thinks of 'Crème de Menthe' and 'Gladiatorial', for example. Since Lawrence saw things in a new way and set them down in a new way, very frequently the small canvas gave him the right dimension for an impression recollected more in excitement than tranquillity. The result is that the miner's death, obvious and awaited, still never fails to compel the reader's attention and unremitting involvement in *Odour of Chrysanthemums*. That sense of incompleteness in the human relation which comes with the knowledge of death is here given an entirely new direction: for the wife looking at her dead husband realizes what a mockery their intimacy has been – she had no *real* knowledge of the man who lies dead before her and to whom she has been married so long. This is perhaps part of 'the mystery of the flame forever flowing' previously referred to.

It is this intense individuality which gives the work of D. H. Lawrence a transcendent value. At the same time, it would be foolish to deny that he has limitations. Some of his work is over-written, partly a result of his aim to demonstrate the ingenuity and complexity of the human mind. Sometimes his style is slipshod, giving the impression of hastiness in composition, or it is conversational, with vivid metaphors alongside slangy platitudes, as in *The Virgin and the Gypsy*. But Lawrence unquestionably breathed life into the English novel, wrote many stories of arresting interest and lasting worth and much poetry which is way ahead of its time in form and content.

Lawrence has often been seen as a restless and unhappy man. Perhaps we should remember his health – he was badly ill with chest trouble while teaching at Croydon – and the constant tension and aggravation he suffered over the publication of much of his work. He suffered too through the war and through his mother's death and the decision to run off with Frieda: it is hardly surprising that one pictures a man worn from without and within by driving passions, some of which were exorcized by his writing, his wife, his travelling life. Yet if one reads Lawrence's early letters it can be seen how close to common everyday humanity he was, and how free from anger and affection in some respects. In such letters Lawrence reveals his sense of insecurity, a strong core of loyalty to family and friends, a love of children and an impetuosity which is endearing.

Lawrence writes, too, of his work, telling Edward Garnett of his 'immortal Heinemann novel, *Paul Morel*'. He displays a detailed knowledge of fiction, both contemporary and traditional; Lawrence's mind as well as his instinct showed him how to shape his own novels and stories. There is some emotional over-praising and blaming in *The Collected Letters*, together with some astute comments which give a valuable insight into his own feelings. He tells Rachel Jennings 'read *Anna Karenina* – no matter, read it again, and if you dare to fall out with it, I'll – I'll swear aloud,' while to Jessie Chambers he wrote, 'I often think Stendhal must have writhed in torture every time he remembered *Le Rouge et Le Noir* was public property.' Lawrence read widely and deeply – witness his comments on *Oedipus, The Trojan Women* and *The Bacchae* – but he wrote with superb independence and directness. There are more complete novelists than Lawrence, novelists who have perhaps paid fuller attention to form and structure and to the 'literaryness' of their works, but for sheer individuality of utterance Lawrence is without a peer. It is typical too of his unswerving integrity that when *The Rainbow* was banned in 1915 he asked that Henry James, the grand old man of English-cum-American Letters, should read it and indicate whether he thought it should be banned or not. It must be observed here that no two novelists could be farther apart in aim and practice than Lawrence and James.

Lawrence is no great delineator of manners, conventions, sentiment, romance or even of the wider social life of his time, which so many writers take as their natural material. But in capturing and presenting the impulses and instincts of individuals in intimate conscious or unconscious contention or consummation, he is unsurpassed in his vibrant and uncompromising indentification. He is perhaps the greatest novelist of this century, significant indeed for our own time, which takes the artificial and materialistic for life and grows steadily away from life as a result. Lawrence is the life-force exemplified in his best works, and often young readers respond to him because he cuts through, and cuts out, all hypocrisy and so-called 'civilized protections'. As we get older our lives are sometimes constricted by conventions which we would not dare to flout. Lawrence flouted most of them and showed they were made of sand; courage and genius can do no more.

The Rainbow and *Women in Love*

The two novels were originally one, as far as we can gather from Lawrence's letters, the title being *The Sisters*. *The Rainbow* (called initially *The Wedding Ring*) was finished in 1915 and published in September. Two months later it had been withdrawn from circulation and an angry and bitter Lawrence began writing *Women in Love* the following year. As with *The Rainbow*, there was considerable re-writing. It was not published until 1920.

While he was at work on *The Wedding Ring*, Lawrence wrote that he saw himself as a passionately religious man, 'and my novels must be written from the depths of my religious experience'. He did not mean this in the Christian sense, rather he believed in the life-force and in man's ability to discover new depths in himself. At the same time he was bitterly cynical about the war:

> . . . in the world of Europe I see no Rainbow. I believe the deluge of iron rain will destroy the world here, utterly: no Ararat will rise above the subsiding iron waters.

And he adds, 'There is another novel, sequel to *The Rainbow*, called *Women in Love* . . . This actually does contain the results in one's soul of the war: it is purely destructive, not like *The Rainbow*, destructive consummating.' Later, he was to observe that the two novels should be regarded as 'an organic artistic whole', but in his foreword to *Women in Love* in 1920 he referred to it as 'a potential sequel to *The Rainbow*'.

The Rainbow deals primarily with three generations of Brangwens, exploring the intimate complexity of their relationships. Certain incidents look forward to or link with, in imaginative association, unusual, graphic or startling incidents in *Women in Love*. Will and Anna are in conflict, eruptions of passion occur which are either consummation or destruction or both. The pregnant Anna dances naked (think of a comparable sequence or sequences in *Women in Love*). The passion of rejection between Anna and Tom Brangwen again has its equivalent in Ursula's confrontation with her father when he is greatly angered by her hesitation over marrying Birkin and, before that, in her actually entertaining marriage with Birkin. Strong feelings, impulses, irrational and blinding emotion, these are the stuff of both novels. The reader of *Women in Love* will obviously look back at the presentation of Ursula in *The Rainbow*. Her teaching experiences are vividly portrayed, while her affair with Skrebensky is impassioned and wasting, not dissimilar to Gudrun's affair with Gerald in *Women in Love*. In *The Rainbow* Gudrun hardly exists as a character, but by the end, after her survival of her affair with Skrebensky, Ursula has to move forward into life.

Lawrence's over-riding concern in both books is his exposure of the many strands, conscious and subconscious, in sexual relationships. There is no doubt that the war explains much of the bitterness in *Women in Love*, but the rule of the machine age also concerns Lawrence deeply. The style of *The Rainbow* has much in common with that of its sequel, though his use of repetitive, reiterative sequences which are biblical in tone and cadence and establish a religious continuum, are much more marked; he was, after all, dealing with the generations of men upon the face of the earth. The area is richly conjured, the sexual rhythms and natural description vying with each other for pride of place. At the end of *The Rainbow* Ursula is on the edge of new experience. Taken with Gudrun's in fairly equal measure, *Women in Love* is the exploration of that experience. It is also the exploration of contemporary life.

Chapter commentaries, textual notes and revision questions

Chapter 1 *Sisters*

The unusual quality of the sisters Gudrun and Ursula Brangwen is established by their conversation and the obvious contrasts between them. Ursula appears withdrawn and sensitive, while Gudrun is challenging, savouring experience, almost predatory. Both feel, however, that they are moving towards a marriage which may be a trap to stifle the independence they both value. They have obviously grown away from their father, probably because he has settled into a dull provincial existence. The walk to watch the wedding is a challenge which Gudrun feels she must face; she is exposing herself to the almost satanic power of a place from which she has escaped for several years, and she finds this degrading and unnerving. The description of the girls and the area is vivid and intimate. There is some beautiful, casual observation. Notice how Lawrence quickly brings the sisters into imaginative interaction with the Crich family, and, through them, with Birkin, and how these characters are presented externally – observed by the sisters – and internally via their thoughts and intense feelings which pass beyond thought. This first chapter therefore brings the main protoganists of the novel together. Class divisions are seen in the mockery of Gudrun, who rebels by refusing to enter the church. Notice too how we switch from the consciousness of one girl to the other. The focus on the eccentric Mrs Crich in her lonely monomania is particularly revealing. Equally revealing is the perspective on another eccentric (and certainly predatory) woman, Hermione Roddice. Hermione's predilection, for men in a man's world is established at once. Yet Hermione too is suffering. Already we register the atmosphere of conflict which is one of the running themes of the novel. There is a brief retrospect on the relationship between Hermione and Birkin. The description of the bridegroom's late arrival introduces a mixture of the comic grotesque and the insistently sensual ('his supple haunches working like those of a hound'). Interesting too are the descriptions of Birkin and of Ursula's reactions to him. Already the emotional movement of the sisters towards Gerald and Birkin is evident. There is strong fascination and a potent stress on intensity of feeling, but note that Birkin endures rather than enjoys the physical contiguity of Hermione.

sisters of Artemis rather than of Hebe The first the goddess of chastity and of hunting, the second the goddess of youth and Spring in Greek mythology.
reculer pour mieux sauter To step back in order to get a better take-off.
shameless . . . ashamed . . . ashamed Typical Laurentian stylistic effect – repetition of a word or its variants for emphasis.
moleskins The fine-piled cotton fustian used for men's hard-wearing trousers.
'His totem is the wolf' The emblem of his type, i.e. predatory, destructive.
in the Rossetti fashion After the realistic/romantic style of painting of Dante Gabriel Rossetti (1828–82), the pre-Raphaelite artist.
Kulturtrager Upholder of culture.
this strange, sharp inoculation . . . Vivid metaphor, its emphasis on instinct and intuition.

Chapter 2 *Shortlands*

There is a loving description of the Crich home, but soon the perspective shifts to Gerald, his display of social ease and his need to exert authority. The atmosphere of confusion in a family gathering like this is conveyed. Mrs Crich's eccentricities are strongly pronounced as she engages Birkin in conversation. Her eyes have the hint of madness, her slovenliness and dirtiness reflecting an unwillingness or perhaps inability to conform. Birkin's sensitivity to the situation is obvious, as is his intolerance of the influence, the intrusion, of people. Mrs Crich spells out Gerald's isolation, even alienation; there is pathos in her expressed wish that he needs a friend. With dramatic suddenness Lawrence reveals the reason for this – he has accidentally killed his brother. Gerald's assertion of authority through the conch is another strange, grotesque manifestation. Though they have position (and money), there is certainly something different about the Criches. The emphasis on the various play of moods in Mrs Crich is fascinating, and we anticipate positive action when we are told that 'a sullen eagle look was on her face'. Competition and emulation form the basis for the conversation between Birkin, Gerald and Hermione. Hermione shows her murderous potential, later translated into action in the paperweight incident in Chapter 8. Birkin realizes that he has been provocative, perhaps a result of his dislike of these social occasions. The conversation about man and nation contains an oblique rejection of the First World War. There is an edginess about the atmosphere, while the ensuing conversation between Gerald and Birkin shows Birkin's belief that 'it takes two people to make a murder', an important statement in view of events. We feel the suppressed violence beneath the social surface. The mystical intensity, the love-hate fusion between Birkin and Gerald, is fascinating and consuming.

'Am I my brother's keeper? . . .' Cain's cry See Genesis 4: 1–16.

Chapter 3 *Classroom*

This contrasts immediately with the preceding chapter, but we get the authentic feeling of the classroom. Ursula, despite her trance-like obsession with what she is doing, reveals her inclination for Birkin by her reaction to his unexpected entrance. He immediately responds to what he senses is her mood. By a subtle innuendo Lawrence makes it clear that the catkins and the crayoning carry sexual implications which charge the atmosphere enveloping Birkin and Ursula. The drama is heightened by the unlikely entrance of the predatory Hermione. Yet, strangely, the sexual atmosphere is not diminished but enhanced, for Hermione brings with her her own quality of mystic absorption. Hermione's account of Gudrun is interesting – she praises her carvings in their primitivism; she also emphasizes the fact that Gudrun is interested in 'little things' (perhaps a forecast of her being fascinated by Loerke). Conflict erupts between Birkin and Hermione as she tries to probe motivation: soon she is caught up in a rhapsodic condemnation of the mind, which she considers death – 'the dead quality of knowledge'. But Birkin is quick to respond, pointing out that the animalism that she wants 'you want . . . in your head', in other words, she wants to observe herself. Ursula is frightened by the intensity of passionate hatred between Birkin and Hermione. In his attack on her, Birkin tells Hermione that her passion is a lie, but we notice that such is his sensitivity that he is ashamed of his own viciousness towards her. For Birkin, as he admits to Ursula, pure sensuality is all – 'the great dark knowledge you can't have in your head'. Although Birkin is conscious of being mocked by the women (who are made uneasy by his revelations), Hermione exults in the assurance that Ursula is her rival for Birkin. Again the theme of conflict is evident, though at the same time Ursula is aware 'of richness and of liberty' in Birkin. Finally her own reaction is to cry, without knowing why, and this shows how deeply her emotions have been touched.

that Lady of Shalott business From the poem by Alfred, Lord Tennyson (1809–92), in which the Lady is imprisoned in a room to weave, seeing life through a mirror. When she steps outside reality kills her.
'***Woman wailing for her demon lover***' From the poem *Kubla Khan* by Samuel Taylor Coleridge (1772–1834).

Chapter 4 *Diver*

The first paragraph gives us the quality of Lawrence's superb natural observation, with its sights, sounds and contrasting colours. Gerald swimming exerts a powerful fascination on Gudrun, while he himself experiences the exultation of being 'immune and perfect'. Gudrun enunciates the man/woman distinction, her main point being that the man enjoys freedoms denied to the woman. This is the core of conflict. The conversation the two girls have about Shortlands shows the changes, in terms of modernization, which Gerald is carrying out. Again the account of Gerald killing his brother is given a weighted importance, here by Ursula, though Gudrun finds her emphasis shocking; still it contributes to Gerald's fascination. The difference between the sisters is underlined by Ursula's concentration on unconscious will and desire, which Gudrun rejects. Ursula shows her resentment – one is tempted to say jealousy – of Hermione after their brief encounter. The comparison of Ursula and Gudrun to a pair of scissors shows their sharpness, their edginess, the fact that they use their tongues to cut out their frustrations. The monotony of their lives is apparent, though Gudrun enjoys her own cleverness.

Nibelung Legendary race of dwarfs in Germanic legend.
Dorothy Wordsworth (1771–1855) The devoted sister of William, who used material from her journals in his poetry.
Jane Austen (1775–1817) Celebrated ironic and moral novelist, author of among others, *Pride and Prejudice*.
pour moi elle n'existe pas For me she doesn't exist.
infra dig Unbecoming, beneath one's dignity.
à terre Down-to-earth, unimaginative.
Corneille (1606–84) The great French classical dramatist.
Je m'en fiche I don't care.

Chapter 5 *In The Train*

This chapter focuses sharply on the interaction between Gerald and Birkin: despite very real differences they are strongly drawn to one another. First they discuss newspaper cant. Lawrence's disillusion about the media is evident; the idea of a new gospel for the mechanistic machine age which, in some ways, is represented by Gerald. Birkin is realistic – he thinks people merely want novelty. He proceeds to launch his attack on the lies and images of modern life, his conflict with Gerald apparent, since the latter lives for his work. He even expresses his hate. But he also expresses his need for the finality of love, something which Gerald does not want. Birkin has already denied the existence of God. Gerald is fascinated by Birkin, but the latter goes into his own absorbed state, wishing that mankind would pass away since it has done all it had to do. His account of his London connections is cynical, but Gerald is drawn towards the prospect of loose, Bohemian behaviour. Note that London – far from nature – depresses Birkin.

like in a Brocken mist Brocken is the highest of the Harz mountains in Saxony, the supposed scene of the witches' revels on Walpurgis night.
Sodom Twinned with Gomorrah in terms of wickedness. See Genesis 18: 16–33.
Pompadour Since it is sexually inviting and promiscuous, named after the mistress of Louis XV of France, Madame de Pompadour (1721–64).
Where the quiet coloured end of evening smiles... From the poem *Love Among the Ruins* by Robert Browning (1812–89).

Chapter 6 *Crème de Menthe*

The atmosphere – trivial, degraded, Bohemian but without joy – is brilliantly captured by Lawrence. The chapter is satirical, with Halliday as the chief butt, though Minette too is seen clearly in her pointless existence. We get the sense of a trap: there is sexual, perverted, craving sensation with an absence of any real emotion. We note that Birkin is diminished in such surroundings, though by contrast Gerald grows in power at the prospect of sexual gratification – fulfilment as such would be impossible. Minette is fully described, and we share Gerald's movement of attraction towards her. Halliday is caricature, grotesque, green, hysterical, a man (just) of easy moods, simulated for effect. His row with Minette exemplifies an almost effeminate pettiness. Note Gerald's fear of being locked up or restrained in any way, (p.73). Gerald's sense of power and excitement are fuelled by Minette's story about Halliday and the baby and the delicate way she eats the aphrodisiac oysters. Minette's sadistic violence in jabbing the young man, the flow of blood, of drink and of conversation, all underline the shadowyness and immorality of the Bohemian lifestyle. Birkin is plainly disgusted by Gerald's reactions and his obvious involvement with the girl. Halliday is foolish after just one glass. The taxi-ride serves to make the coming together of Gerald and Minette certain; the arrival at Halliday's speaks of further degradation, made explicit by the presence and the importunity of the servant, the boy kept by Halliday. Birkin opts out of the situation, but the rest of the chapter is devoted to the understanding among the men that Gerald is to have Minette. We get a strong sense of weakness and yet easy pleasure in Halliday, the active connivance of the young Russian, an overwhelming sexual atmosphere, both heterosexual and homosexual, of which they are all aware.

Minette Pussy, tabby, darling (with obvious sexual associations).
in a very small, quick Eton voice i.e. upper-class affectation.
dwy Deary.
unfolded like some fair ice-flower . . . Note the image. It suggests Gerald's later death in the cold, while the image also reflects the strong sexual attraction that Mr Crich feels for Christiana in their marriage. Lawrence is thus giving Gerald a family consistency.
she suddenly jabbed a knife . . . One of the Lawrence's techniques is to indicate the nature of this decadent society by sudden eruptions of violence – this is the first of a number in the novel.
cat Be sick.
this black electric comprehension . . . A subtle friction of electricity, one of Lawrence's favourite images to indicate sexual power and compulsion.
a swell i.e. rich, upper-class.
that she was sitting in child-birth i.e. a representation of suffering as distinct from the simulated feelings of this decadent group.
the Futurist manner The Futurist movement began in Italy at the end of the first decade of the twentieth century – it was a revolution in art against traditional static methods of representation.
turgid with electric force, and his back was tense like a tiger's Note the powerful combination of the man-made and the animalistic in this image.
drowned in some potent darkness . . . Indicative at the same time of corruption, and the night which Gerald fears.

Chapter 7 *Totem*

Gerald's initial tender consideration for Minette is banished when he sees the two young men naked, Halliday obviously delighted at his own flouting of convention. Gerald responds to the 'heavy, broken beauty' in Halliday until repelled when the latter reveals that all he has is a craving for experience (perhaps what Birkin meant in ch.3 by wanting passion and instincts through the head). Birkin appears, and the emphasis is now on the representation of the savage woman in labour. Birkin connects it with art, Gerald with Minette (he is of course reminded that she is going to have a baby). Birkin finds it 'utterly sensual'. When Gerald sees Minette again he realizes that he must leave her. Birkin feels revulsion at the sight of the Arab. The air is strong with sophisticated Bohemian corruption. Worse than that, the corruption and contiguity have generated hatred. There is a strong feeling too that there is no kind of fulfilment in this life, that all is pettiness and misguided motivation.

the unliving furniture Superb unobtrusive description.
a Christ in a Pièta A picture or sculpture of the Virgin Mary holding the dead body of Christ on her lap.
comme il faut Impeccable, absolutely as they should be.
like a flint knife... Note the ominous nature of the image.

Revision questions on Chapters 1–7

1 Compare and contrast Gudrun and Ursula as you have come to know them so far. Which one do you prefer and why?

2 Indicate the part played by Hermione in the action so far.

3 In what ways do you find Birkin an unsympathetic character? Give reasons for your answer.

4 Write an account of the London scenes, indicating the part played in them by any two of the characters.

5 Show how Lawrence creates atmosphere in either the church scene or the scene at Shortlands.

6 Whom do you find the most interesting character in these early chapters and why?

Chapter 8 *Breadalby*

The chapter opens with a description of the house and grounds, of Hermione's insistent presence, the contrast between the two sisters. Yet even here Lawrence is satirical, the characters present (for instance, Alexander) are more caricatures than people; there is 'a canal of conversation rather than a stream'. Birkin is reduced in such company, which we are told 'was mental and very wearying'. What Lawrence captures here very successfully is the intensity of personal feeling and frustration which animates the main protagonists. Birkin asserts that knowledge only exists of the past, and is conscious of raising the temperature between himself and Hermione when he refuses to accompany her on a walk. Hermione's anecdote of the two male swans refers pointedly to the triangular situation. When they return, she is stimulated by her conflict with Birkin, and to 'extract his secrets', but is reduced by their exchanges, by his 'insidious occult potency'. Through the heavy, threatening atmosphere ('anarchistic', 'powerful and destructive') we remain aware of Hermione's curiously drugged state. The dance leaves Hermione fascinated and frustrated, while Gudrun as Ruth and Ursula as Naomi register strongly with Gerald and Birkin respectively. When Birkin dances, Hermione is moved to a deeper hatred. The latter conversation between Birkin and Gerald reveals Gerald's interest in Gudrun and indeed in Birkin himself. Birkin is particularly savage as they talk in dealing with the shortcomings and inconsistencies of Halliday. Birkin is now moved in his turn by Gerald. The next day he tries to analyze Gerald, since Gerald clearly does not know what he wants. Birkin becomes impatient with the company. There is a general consensus to bathe. Gudrun and Ursula watch, and Gudrun is repelled by the reptilian (saurian) associations of the men. The climax of the chapter is Hermione's assault on Birkin, her murderous intent and the goading and drugged state which precedes it. Note that she tries to crush his skull with a lapis lazuli ball, and recall his vindictiveness in Chapter 3 when he suggests that her skull should be cracked like a nut. Birkin's reaction – and his acknowledgement of what he has done to Hermione – is an attempt to cleanse himself of the corruption and sickness within as well as ridding himself of the weight of her passion for him.

like a Meredith hero who remembers Disraeli Lawrence is being satirical about the romantic heroes – larger than life – of George Meredith (1828–1909) and Benjamin Disraeli, novelist and Prime Minister (1804–81).

'Silent upon a peak in Dariayn' The last line of Keat's fine sonnet 'On First Looking into Chapman's Homer', its sestet celebrating Cortez's first overview of the Pacific. 'Silent upon, a peak in Darien.'

***Fathers and Sons* by Turgenev . . .** Bazarov is the nihilistic hero of this book by Turgenev, the great Russian novelist (1818–83). Note that Miss Bradley mistranslates from the French – there is no 'hurriedly'.

Cassandra The daughter of King Priam of Troy: she had the gift of prophecy, but her prophecies were not believed.
Anche tu, Palestra, ballerai . . . Will you also dance Palestra – yes please.
'Vergini delle Rocchette' Virgin of the Rocks.
Naomi and Ruth and Orpah The first the mother-in-law of Ruth (Ruth 1: 2;22); Ruth was the wife of Mahlon, who settled in the land of Moab. Later she married Boaz, her son being the grandfather of David (Matthew 1:5). The third was a Moabitess, wife of Chilion (Ruth 1:4:14).
like a hermit crab from its hole Vivid simile to indicate his intensity and his dissociation from the scene.
'Cosa vuol'dire Palestra?' 'What do you mean, Palestra?'
réclame i.e. advertising ability.
a Botticelli face Botticelli (1447–1510), Florentine Renaissance painter whose figures were serene and beautiful.
'render unto Caesarina . . .' Birkin's laconic parody of 'Render therefore unto Caesar the things which are Caesar's.' (Matthew 22:21).
Integer vitae scelerisque purus An upright man free of guilt.
'Salvator femininus,' A female saviour.
Dionysus The Greek God of fertility, of nature and of wine.
Obermeister . . . Untermeister Over . . . Under, prefixed to master, leader.
as a swimmer struggles with the swirling water . . . Another anticipation of the drowning to come.
Thucydides The great fifth-century BC Athenian historian of the Peloponnesian war.
like Alexander Selkirk (1676–1721) A sailor who was put ashore on the island of Juan Fernandez in South America, the inspiration of Daniel Defoe's *Robinson Crusoe*.

Chapter 9 *Coal-Dust*

As if the Hermione incident were not enough, Lawrence now provides an equally striking one, that of Gerald compelling the mare at the crossing. Again, the effect that this produces on each of the girls shows their different natures. Ursula is appalled by his sadistic cruelty, Gudrun attracted by his power. In a sense, the mare symbolizes her, and this scene anticipates Gerald's coming to her and taking her after his father's death in Chapter 24. Notice the vivid actuality of the sequence. The sexual theme is continued in the countrymen's appraisal of the girls, and particularly in the older man's expressed desire for Gudrun. There follows an account of Gudrun's love-hate relationship with the area. The Friday night experiences are imbued with common warmth and Gudrun's reaction to them expresses the conflict within herself. This is itself a reflection of the restless nature of the protagonists in the novel – each is aware of roots, the immediacy of the past on the present, and at the same time the need to escape, to achieve independence.

pleased with the delicate quivering of the creature between his knees The first of many sexual images.
keen as a sword pressing into her Strongly sexual suggestion – and the indication of a permanent wound too.
that'll have his own road i.e. do what he wants to do.
welly Really, actually.
like a new Daphne, turning not into a tree but a machine Daphne was the nymph in Greek mythology who was pursued by the amorous God Apollo. She was changed into a laurel tree when he attempted to seize her.
the sirens Nymphs in Greek mythology who lured sailors to their deaths by the beauty of their music.

Chapter 10 *Sketch-Book*

The description of the water-plants is vivid and sexually evocative. Ursula is all absorbed consciousness, and so is Gudrun in her sketching, though she experiences a *frisson* when she sees Gerald. Lawrence uses what becomes a commonplace in his imagery to describe the potency of Gerald for Gudrun – that of electricity. Gerald is unaware of Gudrun as an individual yet; Hermione brings emotional and physical discordance to the scene, and Gudrun uses her sarcasm on Hermione. The latter enjoys upsetting the sketch-pad, and Gerald is now directly absorbed in his response to Gudrun. Though he recognizes her hostility and coldness he is compelled by her. Gudrun realizes her own power, and exults in the knowledge that she can reduce Gerald. Both Gerald and Gudrun have succeeded in reducing Hermione.

rigid, naked, succulent stems Strongly sexual, phallic suggestion.
frisson Thrill of pleasure.
the movement of his white loins Further emphasis of the sexual atmosphere.

Chapter 11 *An Island*

Ursula's wanderings bring her, as if by chance, to Birkin. Note how the parallelism in the plot is developed in the fortuitous meeting of both couples. Birkin's simple appeal to her practicality shows the beginning of his dependence (which he would not acknowledge) on her. Ursula honestly expresses her fear and feeling about illness and Birkin his views that mankind is dead, views which Ursula stiffens herself against. He feels that humanity 'is a huge aggregate lie' and is particularly bitter about love, asserting that it is only a part of one's feelings. Further, he sees creation as nature independent of man. Ursula finds that she is responding to the 'duality of feeling' in him, and she is also aware that he is exerting some kind of control over her. The description of the daisies – and they have a symbolic function here of bringing Birkin and Ursula together – is brilliantly poetic. Birkin says that his affair with Hermione is over and we note that he feels that 'freedom' is the most important thing. At that moment they realize that Hermione and Gerald have arrived. Ursula declares her dislike of Hermione, which is at least partly a jealous reaction to the hold she knows Hermione still has over Birkin.

Paul et Virginie The novel by the French author Bernardin de St Pierre (1737–1814).
Watteau (1684–1721) The celebrated French painter and engraver.
Dead Sea Fruit Sponges.
simulacra Mere pretences.
the Salvator Mundi touch Salvator Mundi – The Saviour of the world.
desideratum Something required or desired.
the Ark of the Covenant See Joshua 3:6.
Dervish dance Dervishes were the fanatical followers of the Sudanese Mahdi, who were known to dance in wild circles while in a state of trance.
cotillon A dance with an elaborate series of steps – a brilliantly imaginative usage here.
compositae The daisy family of flowers.

Chapter 12 *Carpeting*

Again an opening with vivid description, this time of the caged canaries singing, perhaps symbolic of the prison of self since they have 'a strange funereal look' when they are covered. Notice how Hermione cuts off all contact with Ursula on the appearance of Birkin. She takes charge of Birkin, rather as one might a possession, and forces him to accept her valuable rug. Later she again exerts her 'dark, convulsive power' by frustrating a row between Ursula and Gerald (over his treatment of the mare, Chapter 9). There is much discussion of the 'dual will', both Birkin and Gerald asserting the need to have control over animals and, by implication, women. There is an interaction of affection, albeit temporary, between Hermione and Ursula, though their agreement seems to be based on the fact that they dislike Birkin's tearing things apart. When Ursula goes home she tries to get Birkin out of her system but does not succeed.

foulard Silk.
Fabre (1823–1915) Celebrated French naturalist.
palaver Talkative fuss.
seeming to accept confirmation from her Note the religious connotation. Elsewhere Hermione is referred to as a priestess.
however man is lord of the beast and the fowl Another Alexander Selkirk echo (see note p.23), this time from the poem 'The Solitude of Alexander Selkirk' by William Cowper (1731–1800).

Chapter 13 *Mino*

Ursula's possessiveness over Birkin is seen in the fact that she resents his having asked Gudrun to tea as well. Her determination to bring things to a head is shown by her going alone. Birkin responds typically, searching for the indefinable as a means of expressing what he wants, which is beyond love, 'beyond any emotional relationship'. His assertion that he wants to deliver himself over to the unknown mystifies Ursula, who thinks in more conventional terms. She feels – and this is what she wants to feel – that he has confessed his love for her. And, by confiding the depth of his idealism to her, in a sense he has. The cat episode, heavily symbolic, follows: it exemplifies the male-female relationship as seen by Birkin, and in a curious way it is an object – or subject – lesson for Ursula. She resists the implication fiercely; over tea Birkin tries to redress the situation by saying that they would be 'two single stars in conjunction'. But in the end he is subdued by her need for the expression of love.

bagatelles Mere trifles.
persiflage Banter, raillery.
belle sauvage Beautiful savage (here, wild cat).
tell it to the Horse Marines i.e. I don't believe you.
Wille zur Macht i.e. an assertion of power.
rapport Sympathetic feeling for.
you've dished yourself i.e. you've given yourself away.

Chapter 14 *Water-Party*

This long chapter emphatically underlines sexual themes: passion, death, fear, mystery, isolation, and the power of nature, and marks a number of distinctive phases. The Crich entertainment underlines the class differences. There is some good comic interaction between the Brangwen parents and the two girls, though there is an edge too of anger and potential violence which anticipates Ursula's later break with her family, largely because of the conflict with her father. Birkin puts on his social air, is kind to Mrs Brangwen, while Gudrun remains acutely aware of the social differences in the company. The steam-launch idea exasperates her, and she reveals her own snobbery in her account of the trip on the Thames. Gerald, however, is roused by her presence. She shows her gratitude when he agrees to let her manage a light canoe. There is some emphasis on Gerald's injured hand, but the two girls going off together and bathing naked is symbolic of their own (temporary) freedom. There follows their singing and dancing, mystic expressions of their individuality. The grotesque scene with the cattle is again emphatic of the differences between the two girls – Ursula fearful and singing irrelevantly, Gudrun dancing and compelling the animals, tasting fear and ecstasy at the same time.

With the arrival of Birkin and Gerald there is a continued sense of climax. Gudrun's wild behaviour exerts a fascination on Gerald, and she is master of the situation – particularly when she strikes him lightly (note the parallel with Mino and the stray). Gerald confesses his love, which is really his fascination. Meanwhile Birkin teases Ursula, putting forward his idea that they – and all others – are 'flowers of dissolution'. He is stressing the importance of the cycle of creation, that one has to pass through corruption in order to be reborn.

The lantern sequence brings them all together into a kind of ecstatic harmony. Gudrun's rowing of the canoe with Gerald exemplifies her power, but just as they are drifting into intimacy the whole temperature of the narrative changes. The child's cry and the desperation which follows are terrible with tension, though while this is happening Gudrun looks with full and fascinated sensuality at Gerald, who 'was not like a man to her, he was an incarnation'. Gerald's reiterated diving shows his strength and his fear; there is a terrible pathos between father and son, Birkin shows his will and his practicality, and afterwards a terrible and realistic appraisal of what death is. He and Ursula come together in a blinding sexual communion. Afterwards he tries to help Gerald but the latter – deep in his obsession and guilt – associates his own killing of his brother with Di's inadvertent killing of the young man. Ursula is now passionately in love with Birkin.

like a painting from the Salon Annual exhibition of contemporary artists' pictures held in Paris.
'Regarde, regarde ces gens-là . . .' 'Look, look at those people there. Aren't they incredibly childish?'
gabies Fools.
'Un peu trop de monde' i.e. a little too many for my liking.
Annchen von Tharau Title of a German folk-song.
Dalcroze (1865–1950) Swiss composer and teacher of eurhythmics.
'Way down in Tennessee . . .' An appropriate choice of song – Gudrun is bent on travel.
the light fantastic The echo is of *L'Allegro* – 'Come and trip it as ye go/On the light fantastic toe' by John Milton (1608–74).
Cordelia The ill-starred heroine of Shakespeare's *King Lear*.
He had killed his brother when a boy . . . Another reminder, and in view of what happens almost immediately, it underlines the fated nature of the Criches.
ignis fatuus The will o' the wisp, light seen on low marshy ground.
Aphrodite In Greek mythology, the goddess of love.
in toto Completely.
fleurs du mal Flowers of corruption or evil, and also the title of the celebrated sequence of poems by Charles Baudelaire (1821–67).
Herakleitos The Greek philosopher of Ephesus, sixth century BC.
One Hamletizes . . . i.e. talks too much – Hamlet was given to soliloquies, the most famous of which is the one which begins 'To be or not to be . . .'
at outs i.e. at odds with one another, divided from each other.
'She killed him' Once again the echo, here of Gerald's own 'crime' in killing his brother.

Chapter 15 *Sunday Evening*

Ursula's reaction to events and to her love for Birkin is an intense death-wish – she despairs of the commonplace week lying before her. But she is awakened into life with the arrival of Birkin, though he realizes that she is separate from him. Notice how Lawrence, despite the intensity, captures the naturalness of the children's reactions to the visitor, who himself responds with tenderness. Ursula, however, in her changed mood, abuses Birkin for not taking care of his health. This reveals Ursula's real state of mind: her restlessness and aggression are direct results of her physical infatuation. She can't escape from Birkin's *body*. Birkin has his own individual reaction to the unwholesome mood of the Crich household after the death. When Birkin has gone, Ursula's reaction is one of hate – but hate is close to love and equally transfiguring. Lawrence here, as elsewhere, uses repetition to convey the intensity of mood.

like Sappho Greek poetess of Lesbos about 600 BC who is supposed to have committed suicide because of unrequited love.
de trop Too much.
Dryad Tree nymph of Greek mythology.
like some crouching idol An image calculated to bring out the difference in Birkin, a difference that involves self-corruption among other things.

Revision questions on chapters 8–15

1 Write an account of the most moving and dramatic incident in these chapters, bringing out the nature of the atmosphere created by Lawrence.

2 Compare and contrast the chapters dealing with 'Breadalby' and 'Water-party', bringing out clearly what they have in common and where they differ.

3 Trace the developing relationship between either Birkin and Ursula or that between Gerald and Gudrun in these chapters.

4 What is the importance of the chapter 'Mino' to our understanding of Birkin's character?

5 Take any scene between any of the main characters and indicate how the dialogue is important to our understanding of the characters' feelings and reactions.

6 Write on the nature of *either* Lawrence's descriptive ability *or* his examination of the consciousness with reference to any sections in these chapters.

Chapter 16 *Man to Man*

Birkin's attempt to come to terms with what he regards as the bondage of love is painful. He rejects marriage and realizes that sex itself is a limiting experience, a separation as well as a coming together. The intensity of his feelings – despair, anger, frustration – make him ill, but he rises from his bed purified and clear-headed. We notice Gerald's protective attitude towards Birkin, whom he loves but cannot quite accept. He confides his feelings towards Gudrun, which he only half understands. He broods on Gudrun's remark that she would strike the last blow – again we feel the prophetic currents of the novel. There is a fatalistic quality in Gerald anyway, and a pathetic acknowledgement that he and his family are not any good at living. There is some vivid description, as when Birkin accuses Gerald of thinking him a freak: his face 'lighted with simplicity, as when a flower opens out of the cunning bud.' The moment of recognition is tempered by Gerald's painful realization that Birkin can live without him. Lawrence is here underlining the disconnection between individuals who think they understand each other. Birkin is contemplating the nature of love between man and man in a spiritual, mystical way. He has made a 'happy discovery' – the blood brotherhood he wants transcends ordinary love. The ideal is expressed simply as 'An impersonal union that leaves one free', and at the end of the novel he refers to this in his final words to Ursula. Ever practical, Birkin points out the difficulties of the Criches employing Gudrun as a teacher for Winifred.

Magna Mater Great Mother.
Mater Dolorosa Sad, sorrowful Mother.
comme il faut Impeccable.
Amazon... Orinoco A pun on the female warriors and the South American river, the Orinoco being the other long South American river.
'Timor mortis conturbat me,' 'The fear of death disturbs me,' from 'Lament for the Makaris' by William Dunbar (?1465–1530?).
Blutbrüderschaft Blood-brotherhood.

Chapter 17 *The Industrial Magnate*

Gudrun conveys her restlessness by thoughts of going to St Petersburg. She seems to go out of her way to reject Beldover, but learns much of Gerald's childhood and background from her conversation with Mrs Kirk. This chapter is important for shedding light on Gerald's character. Particularly interesting is the account of the conflict between the Crich parents. There is a superbly moving account of the slow death of Mr Crich – realistic, sensitive, completely uncloying in its uncompromising emphases. The distance between husband and wife, and the constraints, are frightful to witness, and Lawrence does not spare the reader. Retrospect brings their divisions vividly alive here on the edge of death. She recoils 'from this world of creeping democracy'. The connection in terms of passion and destruction with Gerald is strongly emphasized. Crich's powerful feelings for his wife – 'a wonderful white snow-flower, which he had desired infinitely' – destroy him. The image of the hawk further defines Mrs Crich's predatory nature. The conflict, muted, between father and son is also described and Mr Crich's over-indulgent love for his daughter Winifred. Lawrence shows clearly the swing of the emotional pendulum. As his father begins to sink, Gerald becomes more assertive. At the same time, the father feels that his last efforts must be devoted to giving Winifred more and more – hence the idea of hiring Gudrun as private teacher.

Gerald's educational and social background is investigated in order to trace his development as 'The Industrial Magnate'. His reforms, as he would call them, are spelled out, as is the dehumanization process involved. There is a brilliant evocation of the conflict between masters and men, with Thomas Crich subjugated by the new forces of social power which have destroyed his old religion of benevolent provider for his employees, who have now become politically aware and active. Gerald sees the mining community as a machine, with himself the controlling part. He becomes 'the God of the machine', and henceforth moves towards the complete perfection of it. Gerald's destructiveness as well as his practicality is stressed. He overrules his father, abolishes old systems, makes old-young men redundant, and has his will despite all the hate that is generated. In the process, we are told, he has almost lost his own identity: 'He was afraid that one day he would break down and be a purely meaningless babble lapping round a darkness.' No casual affairs can compensate for this uncertainty and fear; Gerald contains the seeds of his own destruction.

St Petersburg The Czarist name for what is now Leningrad.
a shine on A situation, a row.
raison d'être Reason for living, being.
Homer . . . Odyssey The great Greek epic poet, date uncertain, author of *The Odyssey* which describes the wanderings of Odysseus after the siege of Troy.
three ha'porth o' coppers i.e. a reference to someone insignificant or small, a child.
the be-all and end-all A quotation from Shakespeare's *Macbeth* (Act I scene 7, line 5) as Macbeth contemplates the consequences if he murders Duncan.
ad infinitum And so on indefinitely.
Deus ex Machina Literally 'A God out of a machine', divine intervention.
the sati in India Suttee – the Hindu custom whereby a widow was burned alive on her husband's funeral pyre.
the butty system was abolished 'Butty' – friend, mate. A 'butty' was a middleman in the mines.
A Pussum Mistress.

Chapter 18 *Rabbit*

Gudrun is intrigued at the thought of going to Shortlands, but she also realizes how it will be construed. We note the focus on the child and the mention of her 'irresponsible callousness'. Winifred adjusts herself to the situation, her ostentatious love lavished on her dog. Her drawings are in effect a reflection of her grotesque and potentially wicked character. The initial exchanges between Gerald and Gudrun are self-conscious, but in the sequence with Bismarck (note the very deliberate choice of name) they break through to a recognition of their mutual qualities. Gudrun is determined to battle with the rabbit, which scratches her, and Gerald recognizes 'her sullen passion of cruelty' which, ironically, later undermines him. Gerald overpowers the rabbit and Gudrun, watching him, is aware that she has given herself away, and that Gerald sees into the core of her. It does not diminish his fascination for her. Images of fire and lightning accompany their mutual recognition of their inherent cruelty. Their respective wounds and the rabbit's burst of frenzy symbolize the self-wounding and the passion close to cruel madness which is to be so important a part of the relationship between Gudrun and Gerald. We are told that there is an 'obscene recognition' between them.

like the Bluecoat boys The uniform worn by the boys of Christ's Hospital School, the 'Bluecoat school', founded in 1522.
Bismarck Named after the Iron Chancellor of Germany (1815–98).
Winifred veut tant faire... In rough translation: 'Winifred would very much like to sketch Bismarck – ! All morning we've had Bismarck, Bismarck, always Bismarck!' 'It's a rabbit, isn't is miss?' 'Yes, it's a big black and white rabbit. Haven't you seen it?' 'No, Miss. Winifred has never permitted me to see him. I have often asked her who this Bismarck is, but she would not tell me. Her Bismarck was a mystery.'
'Yes he is a mystery, truly a mystery, (in French, then in German).
'Surely, oh yes.'
'Surely Bismarck is not a king... he was only Chancellor.'
'What is a Chancellor?'
like a macaw Another vivid image.

Chapter 19 *Moony*

If *Rabbit* represents a combination of symbolic power, corruption, cruelty and recognition, then *Moony* represents the madness associated with the moon. What we have to remember, though, is that the moon also represents love, and when we see this the sequence which initially involves Birkin and then Ursula becomes more credible. Ursula's mood before this, her reaction against people, shows how much she really needs Birkin. Her first sight of the moon is conveyed in sharp sentences which underline her mood. Birkin's assault on the moon – and by analogy on his love, perhaps an attempt to destroy it – is both eerie and grotesque. The atmosphere is brilliant with foreboding and madness. Yet the aftermath is of a coming together, not so much sexual at first as spiritual – Birkin is asking her to surrender her spirit to him. He knows however that words are inadequate to convey what he wants. There is an element of mockery verging on hatred in their conflict but Birkin achieves with Ursula the tranquillity he wishes for. He later ponders on the mystical inheritance of the distant African tribes – 'far beyond the phallic cult' – his mind set off by the memory of the carving in Halliday's room. The confrontation with Brangwen shows the difference between the two men. Birkin is contemptuous of the limited language used by Brangwen.

When Ursula arrives home there is a distinctly humorous tone to the situation. Birkin is seized by self-doubt. The latent antagonism between father and daughter springs out, and Ursula catches at her last strand of independence in resistance to both men – the one who has brought her up and the one who wants to take her away. Birkin's reaction – after all, he is nearly put down – is one of extreme rage. Nevertheless, Ursula is afraid of him, afraid of being compelled by his will, and withdraws into herself. The sisters are in harmony – perhaps subconsciously they are in league against the men who would make them subservient. They agree that Birkin tries to force his wishes on people, but Ursula recoils from Gudrun's cut-and-dried view of Birkin. Later she is disgusted by Gudrun's view of nature, which she sees always in human terms. In moving away from Gudrun she moves again towards Birkin, though she knows that he will never fully abandon himself to her.

Cybele Mother goddess.
Syria Dea Syrian goddess.
Dionysic Dionysus was the Greek god of wine.
the ball-rolling scarab The dung beetle worshipped by the ancient Egyptians, the symbol of resurrection and immortality.
Picasso (1881–1973) The Spanish painter, one of the original exponents of Cubism.
She . . . is the cat's mother A phrase which is critical of another person failing to be polite.
like a frog in a gallipot i.e. trapped (a gallipot is a small apothecary's jar).

the *Girl's Own* i.e. a magazine for teenagers.
Lloyd George (1863–1945) David Lloyd George, Liberal politician and Coalition Prime Minister 1916–22.
after the fashion of the nauseous Meredith poem. I have not traced this, but Meredith (1828–1909) published his famous sequence of poems *Modern Love* in 1862.

Chapter 20 *Gladiatorial*

At this stage, with Birkin furious and Gerald in a kind of suspended motion, the two men meet. Gerald has been overtaken by boredom and has no will to do anything. Gerald pins his faith on work and love, to which Birkin adds a third possibility – fighting. They strip and wrestle, and in their contest they reach to the kind of love which Birkin would define as blood-brotherhood. The climactic scene between the two men has puzzled and often offended critics, but although it has overtones of Lawrentian mysticism – the friendship with a man which he himself wanted and which caused him to focus for a time on John Middleton Murry – it is clear in outline. At this particular juncture both men need each other. The physical battle is a release of pent-up emotion, frustration, conflict: and because of their acknowledged bond their fight is a kind of consummation or fulfilment. The physical contact is the ecstatic panacea which frees their minds. The description is so vivid as to make the contest an overpowering actuality, with Birkin's consciousness – and heart – made to register the immediacy of the impact. Lawrence's mystical emphasis is seen in the words 'The wrestling had some deep meaning to them – an unfinished meaning.' Their physical intimacy complements the other intimacies they know they have. Birkin is sensitive enough afterwards to ponder on the contrasts between them. Both men use this opportunity to confess to each other.

Some old Johnny i.e. a wise man (the tone is ironic).
like the eyes of a stallion A suitable image, for we remember Gerald compelling the mare.
a caftan in Bokhara Long-girdled undertunic. Bukhara is a city in Uzbekistan in the SW Soviet Union.
qui vive Alert, ready.

Chapter 21 *Threshold*

Gudrun is caught up in the mixed atmosphere of Shortlands, clearly realizing the implications. The study of the child-father relationship and the spoiled but exceptional nature of the child is superb. Gerald is becoming subjugated to the power of Gudrun. The latter realizes her power, not only with regard to Gerald but also over Crich. She is finely diplomatic with him, acting her part well. The real pathos of the chapter is seen in the slow death of Mr Crich, whose determination to cling to his few personal relationships marks his tenuous hold on life. Winifred running in to see him is poignant with associations of limited time. Gudrun is shocked by his appearance when she sees him for the last time. She is also moved by his concern that Winifred should have a fulfilling life, and by his misreading of her own as happy. In the scene where Gerald and Gudrun discuss Birkin's need for security – 'to tie himself to the mast' – there is some subtle irony in the fact that Birkin is with them at this stage, but driving the car so that he cannot hear what they say. This provokes Gudrun to outspoken criticism of him, another indication of her cruelty.

faience Painted and glazed earthenware.
mauvaise honte Self-consciousness.
the great serpent of Laocoon The latter was the Trojan priest crushed to death by two serpents from the sea.
answers all right i.e. is good enough.
the abandonments of Roman licence i.e. the decadence and lustful orgies, for example during the period of Nero AD 54–68.
why break eggs about it? i.e. why pay much attention to it?
'J m'en fiche' 'I don't care.'
'et puis?' 'And then?'

Chapter 22 *Woman to Woman*

There is the unpleasant surprise of Hermione's arrival at Birkin's. We get the impression that Hermione will just not let go, and the hostility between her and Ursula immediately registers. The description of Hermione centres on her lifelessness and lack of care, she is a 'priestess without belief'. She treats the idea of Ursula's and Birkin's marriage ironically despite her own painful disappointment. She begins to envy Ursula what she considers is her vulgarity. She would willingly embrace the submission which Birkin requires and which Ursula is on the edge of rejecting. Hermione does her best to talk Ursula out of the marriage by indicating Birkin's shortcomings. Ironically, she only helps to clarify Ursula's own thoughts about Birkin. The antagonism between the two women is now very strong. Birkin's entry does not help – he veers between social trivia and an open rejection of

Hermione's views. Ursula feels that she is outside the culture shared by Birkin and Hermione. She is enraged by Hermione's proprietary behaviour with the cat and, though she realizes the effect this will have on Hermione – and probably Birkin – she leaves dramatically.

Mammon The personification of wealth and acquisitiveness.
suckled in a creed outworn The quotation is from one of Wordsworth's sonnets: 'I'd rather be/A pagan suckled in a creed outworn.'
odalisk Eastern female slave or concubine.
as if the pythoness had uttered the oracle Pythia, the priestess of Apollo at Delphi who delivered the oracles = the pronouncements of Apollo.
si jeunesse savait If youth only knew!
fat Fop.
'Il Sandro mi scrive . . .' 'Sandro writes to me that he has heard the greatest enthusiasm, all the youths, the young girls and boys, are all . . .'
'Vieni . . .' 'Come, come here!'
'Viene dire Buon . . .' 'Come and say good morning to Auntie. I remember I remember well – it's not true little one. It is true I remember,is it true?'
parvenue An upstart, someone who has acquired wealth and position rather than being born with it.
'Sicuro che capisce Italiano . . .' 'It is certain he understands Italian – he won't have forgotten the language of his mother.'
'Ecco,il bravo ragazzo . . .' 'Oh, he's a wonderful boy, he's great, isn't he?'
'Ti imparano . . . Bel gionanetto . . . No! Non e permesso di mettere . . .' 'They will teach you bad ways . . . A fine young man! . . . you're not allowed to put your little paw in the saucer. Daddy doesn't like it. A gentleman cat so wild!'

Chapter 23 *Excurse*

There is little doubt now that Birkin wants Ursula, though he is initially overcome by a sense of inertia and indifference. His gift of jewellery is in the nature of a peace-offering to which Ursula responds enthusiastically, but his erratic mood is indicated by his driving. The deep-rooted nature of Ursula's jealousy is seen in her telling Birkin that he belongs to Hermione. She overcomes this feeling, but senses that in accepting the jewels from Birkin she is pledging herself to him. All is peaceful until Birkin mentions that he has to be at Shortlands for dinner to take his leave of Hermione. Birkin and Ursula slang each other, each incensed by the limitations of the other. Ursula has the edge in rhetoric, referring to Birkin's 'spiritual brides', but some of their differences have penetrated her deeply and the result is that she is totally, if excusably, irrational. Birkin in his turn is penetrated by her power; the passing cyclist provides an almost comic distraction. Ursula's action in throwing the rings at Birkin is a considered one. When she walks away, they become for him 'the little tokens of the reality of beauty'.

When Ursula returns her irrational jealousy has ebbed to a childlike submissiveness in which there is something of fear. But soon they are lyrically happy, and when they settle in the inn there is a kind of quiet ecstasy in the discovery of each other. For Birkin it is more than love; for Ursula it is more love than she believed existed. It is as if she has found the fine source of his being, both physical and spiritual. There are strong biblical associations and cadences in the descriptions here, with Lawrence elevating their individuality to a mythically symbolic level. Even after the completeness of their consummation, the meal is invested with a ritual, spiritual significance in their minds and emotions. His suggestion that they resign their posts means freedom for him, but it merely means travel for her. They go off together into the night. Their communion contains all the qualities of the night itself so that the lovers seem to merge with the night and night's particular associations.

In Sherwood Forest The location is reminiscent of Robin Hood with its romantic associations, but it also has the immediacy of a real locale.

Revision questions on chapters 16–23

1 What do these chapters reveal of Gerald in his human and in his working capacity? Refer closely to the text in your answer.

2 Show what the chapter 'Rabbit' tells us of Gudrun, Gerald and Winifred.

3 Write your own interpretation of 'Moony'. Do you find this a convincing sequence or not?

4 How are the differences between Birkin and Ursula resolved? Trace the main points in their developing relationship during these chapters.

5 How important is the idea of blood-brotherhood to Birkin? You should refer to 'Gladiatorial' and to any other parts of the novel which you consider important.

6 In what ways does Lawrence indicate the influence of the past on the present in these chapters? Refer closely to the text.

Chapter 24 *Death and Love*

With one of those transitions which marks the structural cohesion of *Women in Love*, Lawrence moves from images of life to those of death. The emphasis is on Gerald's revulsion and revolt against his father's suffering. This is the manifestation of his own fear, for he wants the death of his father in order to establish his own power and freedom. He moves gradually towards Gudrun whom he sees as his salvation; his fascination for her is strong enough to counteract the death in his soul. He tries to compel her to his will, but we are certain that it is Gudrun who has the power, despite her dread of him. He defines for her the nature of his own battle, the nearness of collapse. Gudrun feels that she is caught in the trap of having to give sympathy, since this is what Gerald craves. It is with the entrance of Mrs Crich that the emotional grotesqueness of the situation is apparent. She sees clearly into her son's neurotic state, even warning him that he will find he has become mad if he's not careful. She sees the potential for disintegration in her outwardly strong son.

Gudrun asserts her independence in saying that she wants to walk, but so commanding is Gerald and so great is his need that she feels his dominance when he puts his arm around her waist. At the same time she is exultant when she realizes how much he cares for her. In one of the most vivid passages in the novel – their coming together under the bridge where Gudrun knows the colliers take their sweethearts – there is an intensity comparable to the preceding sequence between Ursula and Birkin. The location is of importance – for Gudrun and Gerald, in their different ways, have an earthy, common touch which contests with the more ethereal qualities of Ursula and Birkin. Gudrun passes beyond sense into a kind of mystical/physical swoon. An image of death accompanies her passion, a death from which she must be born again into life. The equation of love and death throughout the chapter is strongly felt, just as it is through much of the novel. And just as Birkin and Ursula were separated by a kind of fear – the fear of possession, of ultimate surrender – so Gudrun is also afraid; but hers is combined with delight, for she thrives on danger.

There follows the graphic but superbly economical description of Mr Crich's death, climaxed by Mrs Crich's words to her dead husband, a mixture of insanity and insight. After the funeral and the departure of all the guests, Gerald is left alone in a terrible isolation – we see signs of his future disintegration. He is dogged by fear. His journey is vividly described. There is the macabre description of his route through the graveyard, followed by the comic scene with the tipsy miner (note here Lawrence's fine use of dialect) which gives the reader a false sense of security before the onset of tension. Brilliant, sharp, staccato sentences are an index of his emotional and physical state. His error in entering the boy's room adds to the tension, which reaches an unbearable pitch. We are constantly on the edge of discovery, and even when Gudrun lights a lamp we still feel the terrible insecurity of their situation. Gerald is both child and man, needing the sustenance and physical passion of Gudrun. He is emotionally injured by what he has been through, and she is 'the great bath of life'. But she is 'destroyed into perfect consciousness'. While he sleeps, she remains painfully, resentfully awake, her mind full of conflicting thoughts – she wants him, and yet wishes he would go and, above all, she is intent on not giving away her feelings to him. Her settling into the bedspace he has left finds her satisfied, and he is 'beautifully still and thoughtless'. We are left with the impression that the God of the machine has been reduced, and that although he has been healed here a worse wound awaits him in the future.

the point of a sword of Damocles Imminent danger – from Damocles, who flattered the tyrant Dionysius. The latter saw through him and sat him down at a meal with a sword hung over his head.
It's quite nuts for you? You enjoy it, don't you?
Queer Street i.e. you'll be bankrupt.
upon the field of his living, radio-active body Lawrence has been rightly praised for his natural imagery, but *Women in Love* shows his striking modernity of expression, as in this metaphor.
aside Besides.
lercality Exact location.
tuffy shop Confectioner's.
But an ache like nausea was upon her An indication of Gudrun's separateness this early in their affair.

Chapter 25 *Marriage or Not*

Gerald's anxiety is seen in his contemplation of Birkin's forthcoming marriage to Ursula – he would like to be married to Gudrun at the same time. This is ironic in view of what we know of Gudrun's feelings. He presses Birkin, obviously wanting his approval, but Birkin is not really concerned with 'legal marriage'. Both have the idea – and this is ironic too – that the commitment to such a union is a final one. Birkin attacks marriage as a 'tacit hunting in couples'. It is obvious that he is set against having a home. Birkin also recurs to the man-man relationship which he wants. Gerald sees the alternatives clearly – he could pledge himself both to Birkin and Gudrun (he feels that she is his doom but cannot resist it) but he feels bound to reject Birkin's offer despite the elation that he feels.

'Who for the second shot?' Who will be the other couple?
'that length' That far.
'lambaste' Beat, thrash.
Lord Bacon (1561–1626) Lord Chancellor of England, important philosopher.
Hamlet's to-be-or-not-to-be See note p.28.
pis aller Last resource.
Égoïsme à deux i.e. living for themselves alone.

Chapter 26 *A Chair*

The somewhat sordid, yet attractive, atmosphere of market day is superbly captured. The trap of marriage is symbolized in the contrast between Ursula and Birkin on the one hand and the young couple who *have* to marry on the other. Note the particularity of Lawrence's description here; the young couple are immediately brought to life – physically, sexually, socially. The scene is strongly visual and, in a curious way, timeless. The chair becomes a symbol of oppression – the tie of material things that is part of the marriage trap. Ursula and Birkin's decision to give the chair to the young couple (note Ursula's reactions to the young man whom she clearly finds attractive) is symbolic of their refusal to accept that trap. The interaction between the two couples is handled effortlessly; the dialogue is natural and sharp. But Birkin is still dissatisfied. The idea of a relationship with Gerald still calls to him – he needs a community of fellowship. Ursula points out, rightly we feel, that he is afraid of being alone; she resists his commitment to Gerald.

Jane Austen's England The eighteenth and the beginning of the nineteenth centuries.
a commandment-stone The ten commandments were written by the finger of God on two tables of stone (See Exodus 31:18 and Deuteronomy 4:13).
Rodin (1840–1917) Celebrated French sculptor.
Michael Angelo (1475–1564) Italian sculptor, painter and poet, famous particularly for his frescoes in the Sistine chapel, Rome.
frisson A shudder or shiver.

'Cawsts something to chynge your mind' i.e. you will have to pay for changing your mind.
arf a quid Ten shillings, or 50p in today's currency.
niver whip a dead donkey i.e. don't do anything silly.
'Only warnts legs on 'is' i.e. he wants legs on the armchair.
'The meek shall inherit the earth' From the Sermon on the Mount, Matthew 5:3.

Chapter 27 *Flitting*

Ursula rather enjoys the drama of her announcement that she is getting married the following day. Her father's possessiveness takes the form of rage. Gudrun's coldness, Ursula's cheerfulness, Brangwen's mockery, all these are the stuff of family strife. The blow is the reflex climax of the situation. When Ursula gets to Birkin's she cries, and we realize how deeply she is wounded. Birkin comforts her and, in a lyrical passage of their coming together, Lawrence uses the imagery of flowers. Birkin is overwhelmed with a sense of gratitude – Ursula has rescued him from the brink of age and death.

After their marriage Gerald sees her, and both are aware that they are paying lip-service to his possible marriage to Gudrun. There follows the suggestion of all four of them going away together, but we feel with Birkin that Gudrun was born to be a mistress. When Ursula returns home to collect her belongings, she and Gudrun analyse their past: as Ursula puts it succinctly, 'Not weeping that it's gone, but weeping that it ever *was*'. There is clear evidence here that Gudrun does *not* want the straitjacket of marriage, yet on the car journey we detect an uncertainty, a feeling of a lack in herself. She now switches to the idea that she *does* want marriage, though we suspect that her feeling is born of temporary envy for Ursula. She is bitter when alone. She can't bear the thought that she has been discussed, and she knows too that she is cast as mistress – and that Gerald has a number of mistresses.

mot Witty saying.
amant en titre One worthy to be called a lover.
Vogue The magazine dealing with fashion which is still published today.
Glücksritter Adventurer, fortune-hunter.
'The little grey home in the west' Popular song of the period filled with sentimental nostalgia, hence Ursula's mocking tone here.
'Il faut avoir . . .' 'Be careful not to do foolish things.'
des betises du papa . . . The foolishness of the father . . . And of the mother . . . and the neighbours.

'glad-eye' Encouraging look, wink.
type i.e. loose-living girl.

Chapter 28 *Gudrun in the Pompadour*

This dramatic sequence takes us back to London as Gerald and Gudrun pass through on their way to the continent. Gudrun, we are told, feels compelled to go to the café, disliking herself and the artistic clientele for doing so (note that via Gudrun's reactions we are encouraged to disapprove of this lifestyle.) The first move – of Minette going over to Gerald – is unsuccessful, but it provides Gudrun with the opportunity to display her loyalty to Birkin. Perhaps she is provoked by the fact that she knows that Minette is one of Gerald's mistresses. This betrayal scene – where private letters are read out in public – has biographical derivations, but one must concede that some of the things Birkin wrote, though not fully in context, would provoke humour rather than anything else. The self-destruction element in the letter is, however, common to the main characters in the novel, and is to be pre-eminent in Gerald. Gudrun's action requires a rare courage – it also shows that she feels passionately about Birkin (and that he is foolish). Her rejection of London reflects Lawrence's own.

Fleurs -hic! du mal! See note p.28.
'"surely goodness and mercy . . . Psalm 23 – 'The Lord is my shepherd'.

Chapter 29 *Continental*

This long chapter brings the couples together and, in a terrible sense, takes Gerald and Gudrun apart. Ursula now has wanderlust and does not really come to herself until she is on board ship. The unity of Ursula and Birkin is very real, particularly in the scene on the forward deck when they come together with a physical, lyrical intensity. This sense of fulfilment continues on the train journey. The short paragraphs and rhythmic sentences convey the rhythm of the train.

Lawrence captures the reunion of the sisters in all its excitement through economic, febrile dialogue. When Gudrun gives her account of the Paris party to Ursula, we get the impression that she is taking pride in Gerald's attractiveness to other women. Perhaps, however, she is even now looking forward to getting rid of him. We note that Ursula is made uneasy by all this. The discussion of England contains Lawrence's radical views, with Birkin expressing, though not with great satisfaction to himself, the force of his love-hate feelings for his country. Birkin recognizes that Gudrun could destroy Gerald. There is some beautiful description in the snow scenes, as in 'where stood the last peaks of snow like the heart petals of an open rose'; and the stark, awesome nature descriptions seem to be echoed in the sense of isolation Gudrun and Gerald feel in the bedroom. When Gerald takes Gudrun and reawakens her passion, it is, ironically, a life in death, for he knows that the doom of Gudrun is upon him, and she 'is gone'. He feels her remoteness and she knows it too. But she agrees to socialize, and it is clear that Loerke is an extraordinary character (remember that he is small, a little grotesque, and that Gudrun likes small things). Ursula shows off her singing and is elated, feeling that Birkin may be somewhat jealous of her. So extraordinary are Birkin's transitions of mood that he now feels himself a beggar for Ursula's love. He too feels the isolating coldness of the place, but comes to full warmth with Ursula (note that Gerald does not achieve this with Gudrun). Ursula sees her present success and elation in stark contrast to her past. Meanwhile, at the party, Loerke's interest in Gudrun is so strong as to make him pettish and jealous that she dances with his friend. Birkin and Ursula come together again with a strange licentiousness on his part, to which she submits. Gudrun feels that Gerald should have any woman that he wants – it is another way of cutting herself adrift from him and finding her own will in action.

Gudrun determines to triumph over Gerald, as she puts it. There follows the terrible conflict of wills between them. The incident of the bag shows her desperation that Gerald should not see her weakness, and it also indicates, as he knows, that she will not turn her back on him any more. He is baffled and defeated, and Gudrun wakes in the early morning hard and victorious. Even as she contemplates his strengths and sees, for a moment, how she could rise in the world with him, she knows that she is actually too cynical to care: she has 'touched the whole pulse of social England' and seen that it was all meaningless. She even talks to the sleeping Gerald and he wakes to sustain her almost on cue. Her experiences in the snow send her beyond herself, and she realizes that she is tasting one of the surpeme moments of her life. They continue to pass their first days 'in an ecstasy of physical motion'.

On the day that they have to stay in, the attraction between Loerke and Gudrun, hinted at at the party, becomes clear. Their affinity springs from their love of art. Loerke expresses strong views on art's function in modern life and Gudrun is deeply moved that he should have suffered privations that have forced him to develop his abilities as a sculptor in order to survive. He does not yet know the effect he is having on Gudrun. Interesting, too, is the fact that both the men dislike him. Birkin refers to him as 'a little obscene monster of the darkness'. Loerke has to be alone with the girls in order to communicate. The statuette of the small naked girl is vividly described. Gudrun criticizes it, but she is really doing homage to the little man who made it and resents Ursula's criticism. Loerke in a passion transfigures himself by his definition of the absoluteness of art. The divisions betweeen the girls in their appraisal of Loerke's work begin to make themselves felt. Note how, when Gerald arrives, Gudrun lets Loerke know that she understands how completely he *knew* the mistress-student who was the model for the statuette. There is a kind of intimate triumph and subjection for her at the same moment. The effect on Gerald is to reduce him by the force of this new intimacy.

Ursula wants to leave this snow-bound world which now seems 'unnatural'. The complexities in her love for Birkin and his for her are indicated. Gerald and Birkin have grown apart, with Gerald becoming increasingly tense. Gudrun's gift of the stockings to Ursula is the prelude to confidential talk: she wants to discover if, in going away, Ursula feels that she is turning her back on everything they have shared including, in particular, this experience together in the snow. Gudrun is really probing: she examines Ursula's ideas of making a new world by saying 'to isolate oneself with one other person isn't to find a new world at all, but only to secure oneself in one's illusions'. Ursula fears words and the force of argument: Gudrun advances the idea that love is everything, but Ursula, one is inclined to say, under the tutelage of Birkin, replies that 'Love is too human and little'. After this Ursula is conscious of Gudrun's patronage, and of the fact that she – Gudrun – is constrained by their discussion and the indication of their different visions, their separateness. When we revert to Birkin and Gerald we find that their conversation, inevitably, has been just as intense. Gerald confesses that Gudrun's softness has reduced him, he feels blasted – 'you're shrivelled as if struck by electricity'. Birkin feels the separation from Gerald keenly, perhaps intuitively.

like disembarking from the Styx into the desolate underworld In Greek mythology this was the river of Hades over which Charon rowed the shades of the dead.

'A Bale – deuxième classe?... 'To Basle – second class – Here!'

'Nous avons encore... Encore une demi-heure.' 'We have still... half an hour.'

revenant Ghost.

La vie, c'est une affaire... Life is a matter of noble souls.

whole-hogger Someone who does everything completely.

Tant pis pour moi So much the worse for me.

Kranzkuchen Round cakes with a hole in the middle.

prachtvoll... Splendid and wonderful, marvellous and indescribable.

Reunionsaal Community room.

'Herr Professor, darf ich vorstellen—' 'Professor, may I present—'

'Nehmen die Herrschaften...' 'Would those present like to join in the conversation?'

Loerke Some critics have felt that the name is derived from Loki, the spirit of evil and mischief in Norse Mythology.

'Das war ausgezeichnet, das war famos... Wissen Sie.' 'That was splendid, that was great... Genuinely great... Oh what a pity... Yes, that really is a shame, dear lady. Do you know—'

'Annie Lowrie' 'Annie Lawrie' famous Scots folk-song.

'Wie schön, wie rührend... Wirklich!' 'How beautiful, how moving. Ah these Scottish songs, they have so much feeling. But the gracious lady has such a wonderful voice: the gracious lady is a true artist, she really is.'

Anton Skrebensky Ursula's lover in *The Rainbow*.

Prosit Cheers, your good health.

mene See Daniel 5:5 The writing on the wall, King Nebuchadnezzar's dream interpreted by the prophet Daniel.

Frauenzimmer A beautiful girl.

Parnell and Katherine O'Shea Charles Stuart Parnell (1846–91) the great Irish leader was in favour of Home Rule; he was cited in the divorce case of Major O'Shea as having committed adultery with the Major's wife Kitty. Scandal, and the uncompromising hostility of the bishops, brought him down. He died shortly afterwards.

Mach mir auf... nass Let me in, let me in, you proud person, make me a fire of wood. I'm wet from the rain.

'Alto rilievo' High relief.

Travaillé –... avez fait' 'Work work – and what work have you done?'

Dunque Well then!

Dunque, adesso – maintenant Well now!

'Und Ihr Herr Gemahl...' 'And your husband, how old is he?'

Wissen 'Sie You know.

so ist es That's the way it is.

Nein, sie war kein Modell... No, she wasn't a model. She was a novice art student.

'Lady Godiva' The wife of Leofric, earl of Mercia, who rode naked through the streets of Coventry, her husband having agreed to remit the taxes of the people if she did so.

hübsch Pretty, charming.

The Venus of Milo Greek marble statue of Aphrodite in the Louvre.

Verona, and find Romeo and Juliet Verona is the Italian city which is the setting for *Romeo and Juliet* whose families' (the Montagues and Capulets) feud is the beginning of the tragedy.
the Abruzzi In Central Italy.
Blessed Isles Islands of the Blessed – where the souls of heroes and good men were taken after death.
I don't look before and after . . . Nor pine for what is not. 'We look before and after/And pine for what is not.' Shelley, 'Ode to a Skylark', lines 86–7.

Chapter 30 *Snowed Up*

With Birkin and Ursula gone, Gudrun strives for her freedom, but she is dogged by Gerald's blind assertion of will. She wants to know how much he loves her and provides the killing answer herself, which eclipses him. She reduces him further by saying that she never loved him but merely took pity on him because he was in such a state. When she demonstrates that pity he draws even more deeply into himself – wishing that he could kill her, aware too of the onset of what he feels is madness. Gudrun appropriately sums up the reality of his 'love' in her own mind – 'Try to love me a little more, and to want me a little less.' She then further defines the degradation of his love-making – he wastes her, which is of course a further degradation to him. She persuades him to make love again, but feels that the experience is a kind of death, that it will kill her. He determines to be self-sufficient, but, looking into himself, realizes that the state of self-isolation would kill him. 'It was a state of nothingness.' He can no longer be immune to Gudrun (or to love or life) because he has given part of himself and been wounded. Gudrun too suffers, but she is not prepared to be torn open, torn apart, again. The visionary experience on the peaks at sunset is beauty to her but not to him. She tries to drive him away so that she can take the experience into herself. He threatens her, but she is unafraid and inviolable.

Her days of freedom while Gerald is skiing are spent with Loerke. They are drawn together 'as if they had some esoteric understanding of life'. They enjoy this as much as intimacy, and to Gudrun Gerald seems coarse by comparison. As Lawrence puts it, 'Art and Life were to them the Reality and the Unreality.' A row between Gerald and Loerke gives Gudrun, in her rage and resentment, the opportunity to deliver a body blow to Gerald, by telling Loerke not to call her 'Mrs Crich'. Gerald suffers; but so does Gudrun, who feels his power precisely because she has injured him. When they make love she exerts her will over him: Gerald remains 'remote and candid, unconscious'. Loerke finds her exciting and, strangely, he feels that he is superior to Gerald in his understanding of her and hence in his relationship with her. Subtle thrills of sensation are stressed to indicate Loerke's influence and to underline his contrast with Gerald. Although Gudrun fears that Gerald might kill her, she knows that she must go on. Gerald's limitation, unlike Loerke, is that he is not absolute. Gudrun and Loerke immerse themselves in the past and its artistic richness, avoiding present and future. They are nearing a declaration and Gerald, sensing something of this, begins to loathe Loerke. The rows with Gudrun cause her to will his death, though she can have no knowledge of how effective this is going to be. Gerald still loves her. Gudrun, meanwhile, has the pleasure of knowing that Loerke considers her a remarkable woman. He craves a companion in understanding, and we feel that it will encompass deep dark levels of both artistic and sensual knowledge.

When Gerald returns from skiing Gudrun tells him that she will not go back to England and that things are over between them. Here Gerald acts, for he pretends to accommodate her, but there is deep hatred and the will to kill. When she tells him that she couldn't love him she only just avoids his murderous attack. At the same time, although she wants to leave him she does not want to make him think that she is frightened of him. She consoles herself by damning the conceit and arrogance of most men but naturally excludes Loerke from her strictures. She rationalizes her behaviour by arguing that she is escaping from materialism. She is oppressed by the measure of time. She feels the lack of comfort, experiencing in Gerald's expression of it an addition to her burden. As she thinks of analogies which suit her we feel that she has been seized by a kind of madness – she feels she must escape Gerald but really doesn't know why and is afraid. Meanwhile, Gerald fears the night and being alone. The next day Gerald punches Loerke and Gudrun hits back at Gerald. The latter nearly strangles her, but moves away sickened by what he has become. He wanders up the mountain, desirous only of moving 'till he came to the end' – yet he is afraid of death (witness the scene with the crucifix). One feels that his fatal fall was an *unconscious* desire to end things – that, awake, he would have resisted death.

Mestrovic (1883–1962) Yugoslavian sculptor.
Futurists See note p.20.

peu de rapport Little return.
Cleopatra The legendary Egyptian Queen (68–30 BC) subject of a tragedy by Shakespeare, *Antony and Cleopatra*.
Mary Stuart The ill-fated Mary Queen of Scots, executed 1587 after claiming the English throne.
the great Rachel (1821–58) The great French actress.
Sehen Sie Look, Madam.
'Bitte sagen . . . 'Please don't always call me madam.'
'Soll ich Fraulein sagen?' 'Shall I say 'Miss'?
ne plus ultra Perfection.
borné Limited, restricted.
Goethe (1749–1832) The greatest of German literary figures.
Shelley See note above p.46.
Mozart (1756–91) Celebrated Austrian composer – symphonies, chamber music and operas.
Schiller (1759–1805) German dramatist, poet, historian.
Jean-Jacques Jean-Jacques Rousseau (1712–78), very influential French philosopher, advocated a return to nature, while his *Social Contract* paved the way for the French Revolution of 1789.
Voltaire (1694–1778) Great French philosopher and writer, anti-clerical in attitude: another influence on the French Revolution.
Frederick the Great Frederick II of Prussia (1712–86) raised Prussia to a major European state.
Flaxman (1755–1826) Eminent sculptor.
Blake (1757–1827) Great English poet and visionary.
Fuseli (1741–1825) Celebrated portrait painter.
Feuerbach (1804–72) German philosopher whose chief work on the 'Origins of Christianity' was translated into English by novelist George Eliot (1819–80).
Bocklin (1827–1901) Swiss painter of myths.
in petto In one's bossom.
canaille Rabble, riff-raff.
seltsame Unusual.
religion d'amour Religion of love.
L'amore, die Liebe Love (Italian and German).
chétif Weak, puny, sickly.
baiser To kiss.
soit ou soit pas Maybe or maybe not.
Don Juan Legendary Spanish nobleman who led a dissolute life, subject of a long poem by Lord Byron (1788–1824).
An infant crying in the night The line is from *In Memoriam* by Alfred Lord Tennyson (1809–92).
Hetty Sorrell and **Arthur Donnithorne** Characters in George Eliot's *Adam Bede* (1859). Hetty is transported to Australia for the murder of their child. (Her surname is misspelt, it should be Sorrel.)
comble de joie Heaped measure of happiness.
Zephyrus The personification in Greek mythology of the West Wind.
wohl Your health.

'C'est le sport, sans doute (free translation) This is some kind of a joke.
Vive le héros... Long live the hero, long live ...
Quand vous aurez fini... When you have finished.

Chapter 31 *Exeunt*

Gudrun receives the news of Gerald's death with outward coldness – this is the way people see her. She is moved, but wishes to avoid contact with events, but when she speaks to Loerke – did they will Gerald's death between them? – she is forced to see the barrenness of everything. Lawrence's insight into Gudrun is unswerving, for when she hides her face on Ursula's shoulder she knows she is behaving rightly. But more than this is the secret knowledge she has that Birkin knows she is responsible for Gerald's death. Gudrun knows that Birkin will take the responsibility, will make all the necessary arrangements. The description of the effects of death here is superb – the cold transfers itself to Birkin, who is looking on the remains of the man he loved. So moved is Birkin that he goes to see where Gerald 'went to sleep'. After that he ponders on Gerald's motivation and then on the creative mystery. In the evening he returns to Gerald's corpse and, to Ursula's horror, breaks down. The deep feelings he has for Gerald, the fact that he offered him love – and that that love might have saved him from the final destruction – all this is tragic to Birkin and almost incomprehensible to Ursula. There is also the suggestion that Gerald might live on after death in Birkin. He communicates to Ursula that if he died he would live on in her. But at the very end she can't grasp the two kinds of love essential to Birkin.

'Il est mort?' 'Is he dead?'
Imperial Caesar dead, and turned to clay... This should read: Imperious Caesar, dead and turned to clay,/Might stop a hole to keep the wind away.' (*Hamlet*, Act 4, Scene 1, 235–6).
the Kaiser's The ruler of Germany who was instrumental in bringing about the First World War (1914–18).
'Ich habe es nicht gewollt' 'I did not want it.'

Revision questions on chapters 24–31

1 Write a clear account of the differences which become apparent between Gudrun and Gerald in these chapters.

2 For whom do you feel the most pity, Gudrun or Gerald? Give reasons for your answer.

3 Discuss the view that Chapter 28 ('Gudrun in the Pompadour') could be omitted from the novel without any loss of narrative tension.

4 Show how the climate and the isolation of Innsbruck affects any two of the main characters.

5 Describe the part played by Loerke in the incidents towards the end of the novel.

6 Describe fully the relationship between Birkin and Ursula in these chapters. Is there any development or change in it?

7 What aspects of Lawrence's style do you find most interesting and stimulating in these chapters? You should quote from the novel in support of what you say.

Lawrence's art in *Women in Love*

The characters

Lawrence's characterization, like so much of his work, is unique, particularly in its intensity. For this reason you should read the section involving each character carefully: you will find, I suggest, that just as our own characters are paradoxical, so Lawrence's, in their complexities of interaction and mood, often contradict themselves.

In this section the main characters are treated in the chronological sequence of the novel, so that the student reading the commentary on each can refer easily to the text. Like all convincing characters in fiction, Lawrence's characters *develop*: experience changes them, they become different in some ways as a result of it. At separate stages it is possible to see Birkin as denying sexual love and then succumbing to the ecstasy of it. One can see Gerald both as a dominating and predatory character and as a victim. And so on. The studies which follow must therefore be treated as guides to your own debate about Lawrence's complex characters. They are not intended to be definitive, but they are meant to stimulate you to think about the individual nature of Lawrence's characters and what they represent. You may feel that the characters are too intense, but remember that Lawrence is trying to express the subconscious as well as the outward show in his writing.

Rupert Birkin

His nature was clever and separate, he did not fit at all in the social occasion.

In the *Prologue* to *Women in Love*, which was not printed in the published edition, Lawrence fills in much of Birkin's background. This is interesting in relation to Gerald and Hermione. It is apparent that Birkin was to be Lawrence's voice or, as George H. Ford has put it, 'Lawrence wanted to explore the *possibility* of two ideal relationships, that between Birkin and Ursula, with its redemptive effects on the hero, and that between Birkin and Gerald', and this is of course what he does in the novel. In the Prologue we are told that Birkin and Gerald had met years before and, with a third man, had holidayed together in the Tyrol. They were connected by 'a subtle bond', there was 'a subterranean kindling in each man. Each looked towards the other, and knew the trembling nearness.' Birkin's relationship with Hermione is traced back to Oxford, where she fell in love with him. At that time Birkin wrote 'harsh, jarring poetry' and 'sometimes shallower, gentle lyrics'. At this stage, Hermione can't understand the affection between Gerald and Birkin. Certainly Birkin wants to betray Hermione: 'He, the God, turned round upon his priestess, and became the common vulgar man who turned her to scorn.' Much later, Birkin is to act as best man to the friend who is marrying Laura Crich. This means he will meet Gerald again, and 'the old affection sprang awake in a moment. He wondered what Gerald would be like now.' (The *Prologue* to *Women in Love* was first published in *Texas Quarterly* VI, Spring 1963.)

At this point *Women in Love* as published begins with the chapter 'Sisters', in which Birkin is seen through Hermione's eyes (and in imagination beforehand) and Ursula's at the church where he is helping old Mr Crich. He is incongruous in this situation, though he has a chameleon-like capacity of adapting himself to his surroundings. He is adept at being commonplace, affecting to be at ease. He appears to be possessed by Hermione, and we sense the struggle within him which is to be expressed so strongly later. At the wedding-party Birkin expresses outrageous views like 'People don't really matter' and is then faced by Mrs Crich's request that he become a friend to Gerald. His reaction is to remind himself of Cain and Abel and that Gerald had accidentally killed his own brother. In the ensuing conversations Birkin reveals that he *dislikes emulation*. He shows his independence when he is discussing standards with Gerald. His attraction towards Ursula, the fact of his being possessed by Hermione, comes out in the classroom sequence. But in this scene he shows his *knowledge*, his *imagination* and his *strong sexual awareness*. He indulges the conflict with Hermione, speaking in extremes, such is his fury, his frustration and his sense that he is himself trapped by her. His theory about sensuality is again put clearly – 'You've got to lapse out before you can know what sensual reality is, lapse into unknowingness, and give up your volition.' This, if you like, is the religion of Birkin, and of course the religion of his creator.

Birkin has a weakness – his escapes to London, and his feeling of contempt for the experience. On his way there he encounters Gerald, who is tempted and accompanies him into the Bohemian ethos, and Birkin confides more of his views to him –

his *detestation of contemporary society*, his contempt for those who regard work as the be-all and end-all, and pathetically, his own *need for love*. He also admits that people give him 'a bad feeling'. His attitudes indicate Birkin's *frustration*. At the Pompadour Birkin is in abeyance, quiescent, while the sexual atmosphere builds up around Gerald and Minette. At Breadalby he provokes Hermione, this time with serious results both for her and specifically for himself. Her murderous attack upon him is undoubtedly provoked, and the following scene where he strips and scourges himself on nettles and pine needles and rolls sensuously in grass and flowers is both a cleansing operation and an attempt to break away from the bond of being human – and therefore less than perfect.

His living at the mill-house puts him in touch with Ursula. His assault on mankind continues with the assertion that he would like the world destroyed. His mysticism fascinates Ursula although she rejects his idea on the limited nature of love. He determines to drop his work (he is conveniently independent as regards money) but what he cannot drop at this stage is Hermione. Self-disgust is, after all, a paralytic emotion, making decision-making difficult. The Mino sequence is used by Birkin to show the male in the ascendant over the female. Yet, ironically, it is Ursula who gains the victory by getting Birkin to say what she wants to hear – that he loves her.

Despite himself, Birkin is *all too human*. He also has a degree of easy social charm, which is demonstrated in 'Water-Party'. His *bright personality*, always with a grotesque and unexpected side, manifests itself in the improvised dance he executes before Ursula and the sudden kiss. Birkin can tease when he wants to, and does so here, but basically he is *serious* and *contemplative*. The crisis of the drownings finds Birkin *practical and sensible*.

Birkin tries to deny his own sexual needs, though characteristically and consistently he succumbs to Ursula and is transformed in the process. He himself describes his resistance as 'The old way of love' which appears to him 'a dreadful bondage, a sort of conscription'. He fears 'The hot narrow intimacy between man and wife.' His inward debate fills him 'with insane fury', for he never feels things in halves. It is at this stage that another intimacy develops – that with Gerald. *He feels the need for a relationship with another man,* 'to love a man purely and fully'. He tells Gerald of the idea of the blood-brotherhood and tries to get him to agree to swear their undying loyalty to each other. He is disappointed when Gerald says he needs to understand it better

– but has the good sense to let 'the stress of the contact pass'.

In 'Moony' Birkin's resistance to Ursula, and his surrender, comes to its crisis. His attacks on the moon in the water are attacks on the goddess of love, an attempt to rid himself of the temptations of the flesh and of what he regards as a constricting love. But of course the image of the moon – like the image of Ursula – always returns. He cannot obliterate it. Ursula accuses him of being one-sided, of merely wanting her to serve him. Angrily he uses terms which Ursula can't comprehend (the reader may well sympathize) – 'be glad and sure and indifferent'. He wants a state of stillness with her, and this time his will is the stronger; her attempts to move him into passion and ecstasy are foiled. With an illogical clarity he sees that he must marry Ursula, and with *typical impetuosity* he goes straight to Mr Brangwen. The distance between them is brilliantly indicated, and Birkin knows it. Consequently when Ursula appears he is sarcastic, and when Ursula delays he leaves in a rage. The scene gives us a direct insight into Birkin's character: he is *constantly at odds with himself* but, once his mind is made up, he wants instant results. It is not surprising that, 'After the fiasco of the proposal', Birkin turns to Gerald. In 'Gladiatorial' the two men come together in the intimacy of physical struggle. The wrestling is strongly sexual, the exhaustion equivalent to post-coital exhaustion. The focus is largely on Birkin for him the experience is part of the fulfilment he is seeking. After his 'consummation' with Gerald – and he regards Gerald's body admiringly – he thinks of his need for Ursula. This is not as illogical as it may appear. The two make up the total of Birkin's desires. And again, it is typical of the man that he confides his love of Ursula to Gerald. He buys jewels to propitiate Ursula who, he knows, is setting up a barrier between them on account of Hermione. They need to have the row – Birkin realizes this – before they can come through to a real understanding. After the conflict he quickly moves to the decision which will free them from the restraints of English Society – travel abroad. Their night is full of 'dark knowledge'. For Birkin we feel the exploration beyond the phallic cult has begun.

The question of whether Gerald and Gudrun should marry at the same time is considered carefully by Birkin. Although his tone with Gerald is light, we feel that he sees into Gudrun's heart and knows that she will destroy Gerald. Birkin makes the offer to Gerald of the complete pledge between them – he recurs to it at the end of the novel – but Gerald is not yet ready to commit himself.

Birkin's letters, read out in the Pompadour, are full of *vanity* and *preachiness*; we are inclined to laugh at him – but uncomfortably. It seems that he takes himself very seriously, and one feels that Ursula is a profoundly humanizing influence – that by standing up to Birkin she exacts some comformity from him but also compels him to see sense. On the trip abroad Birkin's *sensuality* – even *bestiality* – are in the ascendant. (Note words like sardonic, licentious, animal, mocking, used to describe this new phase of his behaviour.) Birkin, who has always gone to verbal extremes, now goes to physical ones and Ursula, repulsed and attracted, is here the one who is forced to succumb. Although Birkin dislikes him, he recognizes Loerke's attraction – 'he has the fascination of pity and repulsion for them.'

When he tells Gerald that 'I've loved you, as well as Gudrun' we know that he is bitter about their unfulfilled relationship. The next time he sees Gerald the latter is dead. He is initially practical, 'cold and abstracted', but later he breaks down and weeps. He knows that Gerald should have loved him and in that way he would have lived on in Birkin. Ursula cannot fully grasp this, though he tells her 'I wanted eternal union with a man too', and the final words of the novel exemplify his faith that it was possible.

Though Birkin is *enigmatic* and in some ways unlikeable, he is a *vivid* and *complex character*. He comes to the love of Ursula *intuitively* and almost despite himself, but his search goes beyond her, and that search is frustrated in Gerald's death.

Gerald Crich

He was the God of the machine

In a novel which is called *Women in Love* it may seem perverse or even sexist to deal with the male characters first. I do so because they are the men with whom the women are in love, and because the men tell us so much about the women.

As the God of the machine, which Lawrence hated, Gerald would appear on the face of it to be an unsympathetic character, but this is not so. He is a Nordic type, and this fascinates Gudrun. He is well-dressed, has a 'strange, guarded look' and is 'like a young, good-humoured, smiling wolf', 'sinister' in his bearing. He has immense *social self-confidence*, 'knowing himself the very pivot of the occasion' at the wedding-party. But Gerald's social ease is a thin skin that conceals his *vulnerability*. He killed his brother – the ultimate sin – and compensates by taking over the family and the mines, by *dominating* others. Unlike Birkin, he *believes in emulation*, and his career is a measure of his success. He is attracted to Birkin, perhaps because, unlike others, he tells him some home truths, one of which is that he is a victim rather than a controller. When they go to London Birkin observes that despite his apparent geniality Gerald is 'at bay against everybody'. He is *watchful*, one feels, and perhaps *insecure*. He is honest enough to say to Birkin that he feels there is something wrong with his own life, that he thinks 'It is artificially held *together* by the social mechanism.' This is quite a confession in view of his position. Birkin sees the truth – he knows that Gerald wants to show his enlightenment by liking him, but that he does not want to be forced to take him seriously.

Gerald is *an opportunist*. He rather fancies the idea of taking advantage of Birkin's London visit by joining in the Bohemian group. There is something *sadistic* in Gerald's enjoying his power over Minette. He feels the 'electric force' in himself. The scene at the level crossing with the mare appals Ursula and excites Gudrun. His forcing of the horse, symbolic of the power he exerts over women, the power of sexual compulsion, is apparently part of *his determination always to have his own way*.

'Water-party' provides the opportunity for Gudrun and Gerald to be together. Later Gudrun strikes him, and he feels 'a great gush of ungovernable emotion'. Soon he is telling her that he loves her. The self-control he has employed as a cover has temporarily gone. When the lanterns are lit, so moved is Gerald that we are told he stands by Gudrun 'incapacitated'. He submits further when she takes him in the boat, asking her to kiss him: when she does so 'he stood swooning with the perfect fire that burned in all his joints'. But Gerald feels that *he himself is fated*. Birkin probes this, urging Gerald to get away from the 'millstone of beastly memories round your neck'.

Gerald loves Birkin in his way, and when he is ill Gerald goes to see him. Apart from confiding in Birkin about Gudrun, Gerald reveals his *fatalism*. We feel that Gerald is *a victim*, that he has the beginning here of what is to become a death-wish. He is fascinated by Birkin, and nearly succumbs to the offer of the blood-brotherhood pledge.

Lawrence integrates Gerald psychologically by describing his childhood. Gerald reacts increasingly against his father's determinedly charitable and benevolent attitude towards his employees. As his father fades, Gerald *assumes all responsibility* for the business and *gets things done his way*. Gerald feels compassion for his father, but he doesn't hesitate to undertake all those actions which put the firm before the individual. Mechanical certainty is 'his triumph'. Yet Gerald realizes that he was 'on the point of inheriting his own destruction'. He *acknowledges his fear* to himself: he admits too that it is Birkin who offers some kind of protection from the fear. With Gudrun at Shortlands Gerald has, or nearly has, what he wants. He sees into the heart of Gudrun's cruelty in the incident with the rabbit Bismarck (it anticipates her final treatment of him) and the recognition exercises a strong fascination on him. Gerald comes alive as a result of Birkin's emotional and physical initiative (the chapter 'Gladiatorial' has already been examined). Birkin opens up for Gerald new areas of experience and meaning which he didn't know existed.

With Gudrun later Gerald is 'Blind to her, thinking only of himself.' It is a significant phrase. Gudrun is soon aware of *his separateness*. After his father's death he can stand the thought of another evening alone no longer. His *inflexible determination*, his powerful sexual drive and *the need for love and comfort*, all these are graphically expressed by Lawrence in one of the finest sequences in the novel. After the marriage of Birkin and Ursula Gerald asks Ursula if Gudrun would have him. This shows he is still uncertain. It is at Innsbruck that the divisions between Gerald and Gudrun are revealed, largely because of Loerke. Gerald is elated by the splendid isolation of the place, he is fiercely electric, 'dominated by the constant passion, that was like a doom upon him'. He is supremely happy, ecstatic in their sexuality, but Gudrun is not really with him. He is defeated and subjected later by her laughter at the way he has played with the Professor's daughter. Loerke's small carving, in its perfection, somehow makes him feel barren. Again, before the departure of Ursula and Birkin, he becomes fatalistic, saying (and how ironically right he is) 'There's something final about this.' It is clear that there is hate in his feelings, that he is 'shrivelled as if struck by electricity'. The confrontation with Gudrun finds him murderous after his rejection, for she pulls no punches, defining for him the way that he wastes her. He takes her again, and it is terrible to her.

Gerald *cannot exist alone* after this experience. He delights – that is the word – in the thought of destroying Gudrun. He *withdraws into himself*, seems calm, pure, beautiful. But the subterranean effect has wasted him, and the 'revulsion of loathing' towards Loerke returns with added force. After Gudrun has called him a fool he determines to leave. He *becomes aimless*, except for the desire to kill Gudrun. When he assaults Loerke he is unaware of the effect Gudrun's assault on him – Gerald – will have. It effectively ends his life. Afterwards there is nothing to do but go away from the terrible constriction of her company and his blood-lust urgency, seen in his near-strangulation of her. He goes on and on in a kind of coma, and ultimately finds in the snow the peace of death, though carrying in his consciousness the thought that he is going to be murdered. In a sense he is – murdered by the oppression of Gudrun and *the full force of his own limitations*. As Lawrence puts it, 'something broke in his soul'.

Ursula Brangwen

always thinking, trying to lay hold on life, to grasp it in her own understanding.

At the beginning of *Women in Love* Ursula is twenty-six years old and still caught in the domestic trap. She is *sensitive, uncertain*, sometimes *withdrawn*, but we can see at once from the discussion of marriage between the sisters that she would like to know where she is going. We are told that 'she had a strange prescience, an intimation of something yet to come'. She *loathes her home*, but is frightened of the depth of feeling she is showing. Ursula is *susceptible, impressionable* – the main impact on her is initially that made by Birkin. She is intrigued, piqued, fascinated, finding in him 'a hidden ultimate reserve'. Ursula's *capacity for absorption* is shown in the classroom scene which brings her into direct contact with Birkin. She is disturbed by Hermione's predatory arrival and presence. Ursula is impressed but somewhat bewildered by the force of Birkin's ideas, but she is aware of him all the time, and when she is left alone she weeps, although she doesn't know why. It is an indication of the *depth of her sensitivity*. Ursula has a fear that her life will pass on, and that she will not reach any kind of fulfilment. She is very close to feeling hate, passionate denunciation when Gerald compels the mare at the crossing. She reveals herself completely, much to Gudrun's disgust.

Ursula's key to life is love, but Birkin wants and needs something beyond this and Ursula never really understands this need. She has to restrain her revulsion for Hermione. But she acts *with positive independence* in going to Birkin's – without Gudrun – and takes him on in a debate about love and what is beyond: despite the Mino incident she sticks to her ideas about love (that it is not bondage, for example) – and ultimately *her sexuality*, her *persuasiveness*, her *warmth*, bring Birkin to a kind of submission.

With the crisis of the drowning Ursula experiences another change of mood and the release of the water finds her in her imagination struggling for her own life. Birkin's unequivocal statements about death bewilder her. Again she resorts to what she wants, and when they are walking later she presses herself against him, 'and covered his face with hard, fierce kisses of passion.' The result is that he is 'fulfilled and destroyed'. Ursula has shown her power. Afterwards there is the terrible exposure of her wanting him and yet rejecting Birkin at the same time. Ursula is often uncertain, and the hatred wells up because she feels that she has surrendered herself, and she does not know what she has surrendered to. Birkin goes away and, left to herself, she lapses out.

She is restored by the 'moony' sequence. Just as she cannot shatter his hold upon her, so he cannot shatter her hold upon him by throwing stones at the moon. By chance – Ursula is out walking and sees (and hears) Birkin – they come together in consummation of feeling rather than death of the spirit. Ursula at the time of this is world-sick, in something of a self-mocking state too, really suffering. She wants passion from him, thinking that this is the manifestation of love, but he wants stillness, the peace of loving: and he gets his way.

When Birkin comes to propose, Ursula is withdrawn, though. She is pleased too, revealing a kind of 'vague radiance'. She is here showing her independence: she resents the fact that Birkin and her father seem to be trying to bully her. She also resents the fact that she is seen as merely a physical woman. More than that, her nose is put out of joint (Lawrence's phrase) by Hermione's taking over domestically and emotionally in Birkin's presence. Ursula steels herself against Birkin's overtures, but the jewels dent her armour; she still fights, and in the blazing row which follows *her jealousy, her possessiveness* and *frustration* emerge. She is particularly injured by the fact that she feels her spiritual qualities are not recognized by Birkin. Ursula is a *creature of moods*, and having had her say violently, she comes back to Birkin in a *winsome, appealing* and *loving way*. She wants the reassurances of his love more than anything.

The scene with the chair shows Ursula in a *practical* and *sympathetic* light, though initially she is only 'superficially thrilled' when she finds herself mixing with the ordinary people. Ursula still maintains her independence in argument (note the discussion of the English heritage, for example).

When Ursula announces that she is to marry Birkin next day, her father strikes her. The bonds with her father run deep, and the friction that occurs is because she has outgrown her feelings for him. When she collects her things from her home she is amazed at the sordidness (as she thinks it) she has endured. Ursula is hardly herself now, excited at the prospect of going away but, more than that, *suspended at the thought of a new life*.

On arrival, after being reunited with Gudrun, Ursula is excitied and happy. She delights in the foreign food, and so *gains in confidence* that when she is asked to sing she does it really well. She eclipses Birkin – 'She was dilated and brilliant, like a flower in the morning sun.' She is still pursued by *memories of the past*, but she wants to rid herself of that past and to live in the glorious unknown of the future. She therefore accepts Birkin's change of mood – when he becomes suggestive, licentious, promising obscenities – as a movement into a new freedom, and gives herself up to the sensation.

Ursula has her own uneasy experience with the snow – she feels doomed, and wants to go away. It seems she has absorbed Birkin's idea of the need to travel. She knows that she wants what Birkin calls a new space to be in. She has come to believe 'in something inhuman, of which love is only a little part'. Birkin has succeeded in making her go beyond what she saw as the finality of love. She *has been educated sensually and spiritually*.

With Gerald dead Ursula has to face clearly and undoubtingly the nature of Birkin's needs. When she sees his sunken grief she is filled with revulsion, stricken with horror. She cannot understand what difference it would have made if Gerald and Birkin had sworn the blood-brotherhood her husband so much wanted. Although he reassures her that their love, their being, will not end with death, Ursula, in that curious *obstinacy* she often has when faced with what she can't comprehend, says 'You can't have two kinds of love.' It is that statement which convinces us that although Ursula has developed in terms of the education of the spirit, the feelings, the mind and the flesh, she has still not reached the 'beyond love' which Birkin himself believes in and wants.

Gudrun Brangwen

Her look of confidence and diffidence contrasted with Ursula's sensitive expectancy . . .

Gudrun is *the more colourful* of the sisters, especially where dress, exemplified by her various-coloured stockings, is concerned. She is *talented*, her carvings small but original, expressive, perhaps somewhat twisted. They prepare us for her interest in Loerke and her *intense involvement in the art debate*. She makes it clear from the outset that she *half despises herself* for coming home. Gudrun is very attractive *and knows it*. Yet in their first passing through the groups of young miners she clings to Ursula, suffering the looks and the remarks of the men. It puts her out, and she refuses to go into the church.

Gudrun, perhaps aware of her own strength and a certain cruel streak, is drawn immediately to Gerald. She believes that 'His totem is the wolf' but she is so fascinated that she determines to know more of him. She is furious at not having the same freedom that Gerald enjoys. When they visit Breadalby, Gudrun admires it from an artistic point of view, but she resents it as well. Birkin tells Gerald all about Gudrun – her talent and her travelling life. He says too that Gudrun won't give herself away, that she is always on the defensive. She does give herself away, however, when Gerald compels the mare. She looks at him 'with black-dilated, spellbound eyes'. She almost faints when she sees the blood on the mare's flanks, but she throws the gates open, and screams at Gerald from the intensity of her reactions.

We are told of her Friday evenings with Palmer, and we realize that Gudrun is *in conflict with herself*. On the one hand she wants to be in direct contact, part of, the sensual mass of people; at other times she rejects them, and loses herself in her work. Her account of the Thames river trip to Gerald shows her rejecting commonness again – it shows too her strong sense of class differences.

When Gerald arranges the picnic for them Gudrun is more than grateful. She takes the canoe and *acts the part* of being a 'childlike, clinging woman' which she thinks Gerald will appreciate. In the sequence with the cattle, Gudrun is indulging one of those transitions which make her behaviour *unpredictable, eccentric,* sometimes *cruel,* sometimes *mystical*. At the thought of touching the cattle she experiences 'fear and pleasure'. The words aptly define her mixed response to Gerald later. When she strikes Gerald here it is expressive of her feeling of 'deep violence' against him; but she is so in control that 'with confident assurance' she tells him that she will strike the last blow. She does. Her impassioned feelings assure her 'that she would never go beyond him, he was the final approximation of life to her'.

Gudrun *always has strong views.* After the death by drowning she attacks the display of public grief. She is predictably offended by Mrs Kirk's tone and the details she supplies about Gerald's early life. She is caught up in the circumstance of Mr Crich's wish to take care of Winifred; Gudrun goes to Shortlands knowing clearly that 'it was equivalent to accepting Gerald Crich as a lover.' She handles the situation with Winifred well, but the Bismarck incident reveals 'her sullen passion for cruelty' which gives Gerald some insight into her. She feels her own power with regard to old Mr Crich; she learns to play up to him.

In a revealing conversation with Gerald she expresses a distaste for marriage. Again, Gudrun is in conflict with herself. But 'a stricken look' rouses Gerald. When he walks home with her and puts his arm around her waist, she feels herself taken. She is at one point querulous in asking him how much he cares for her. But when he takes her to the arch – and that other part of Gudrun can associate imaginatively with the colliers taking their girls there – she is exultant in being made love to by the master of those men. She relaxes, she melts into him, swoons, and then awakens to the reality she has temporarily pushed away – the reality of Gerald – 'who was he? He was the exquisite adventure, the desirable unknown to her.' The conflict is terrible, intensely spelled out, for he is the 'enemy' but he is also 'white fire'. She finds him *beautiful.* But in a telling imagery sequence Lawrence conveys the force of her reaction in all the terrible paradox of its being:

> . . . her soul was destroyed with the exquisite shock of his invisible fluid lightning. She knew. And this knowledge was a death from which she must recover. How much more of him was there to know? Ah, much, much, many days' harvesting for her large yet perfectly subtle and intelligent hands upon the field of his living, radio-active body.

Her reaction is to stay away from him. But by now Gerald needs her desperately, and Gudrun is taken almost despite herself. Gerald's journey in anguish and lust finds her warm and responsive after her initial distaste and fear. Later she is 'destroyed into perfect consciousness'. As the night draws on she longs to send Gerald away, to be free from this omnipresent demand. As 'this night of eternity' draws to an end, her main feeling is one of relief. Later she is sick with terror in case he should begin to make love to her again.

Her splendid scene at the Pompadour is her farewell to England. She is *brave*, though trembling afterwards, and bent not merely on retrieving Birkin's embarrassing letter but on showing Halliday, Minette and company what they really are – verbal and emotional parasites. Abroad, she gossips to Ursula, *delights in her freedom* from England, exults in Gerald's attractiveness to other women, and is drawn to, and fascinated by, Loerke. But she is apart from Gerald too, and recoils from him, subjected and torn by his wanting her so much. She is afterwards remote and childlike. Inwardly she is in turmoil. She has her temptations, thinks of giving in and pictures her future with Gerald and the kind of life she would lead with him. She sleeps fiercely, independently, is cynical in her appraisal of social advencement. So attracted is Gudrun to Loerke that when the latter refers to Gerald as her husband she denies him, thereby cruelly humiliating Gerald. She pays Loerke homage, looks into his eyes with a flaming look, for she understands not only his art, but the dark side of his nature, which fascinates her.

The pressures of Gerald's love determine her to begin her fight for freedom. She goes about it cruelly, telling him that she felt pity for him but never love. Gerald finds a 'diabolic coldness' in her. She calls him crude in his wanting of her, tells him that he breaks her and wastes her and then, in a typical transition of repentance and regret, she comforts him, only to be anguished in his embrace with the sense that she will die if this goes on. She understands Gerald's intentions so well, she is so cunning, that she is able to avoid him. She becomes depressed at the thought of Shortlands, of the monotony of life, of being reduced by time and place. And she wants just 'to be wafted into an utterly new course, by some utterly unforeseen event, or motion'. In the final sequence before Gerald's death, she responds to Loerke's teasing and mockery but is galvanized into her assault on Gerald by the latter's assault on Loerke. Afterwards she forces herself to write to Ursula and Birkin, feeling what she calls the barrenness of the tragedy. But when Ursula arrives Gudrun puts on the 'right behaviour'. Within there is 'the cold devil of irony that froze her soul'. She is ironic in her appraisal of what has happened – 'A pretty little sample of the eternal triangle!' That is how people will see it, and Gudrun is content that they should do so. She is *enigmatic* to the end, a vivid evocation of a woman *unable to accept a conditioned role:* but her independence is frightful in its intensity.

Hermione Roddice

Her long, pale face, that she carried lifted up, somewhat in the Rossetti fashion, seemed almost drugged, as if a strange mass of thoughts coiled in the darkness within her . . .

Hermione is both *impressive* and *oppressive.* She is *intellectual,* heavy, 'had various intimacies of mind and soul with various men of capacity'. Lawrence's irony plays over her throughout – for she is 'a medium for the culture of ideas'. In practical terms she *possesses* Birkin. Their arguments – he representing instinct, she representing 'the head' – are laced with personal consciousness and his resentment of their mutual position. The first scene in church shows just how unswerving Hermione is in her determination to appropriate Birkin both physically and emotionally. We are told that she is 'rapt', 'triumphant' and 'demoniacal'. On occasions she contrives to agree with Birkin. Always she is drugged in manner, but when she comes into the classroom we see just how strong her possession of Birkin is. Here they do argue, mainly because of Hermione's idea of the children being 'roused to consciousness'.

Hermione is very conscious of her class-superiority. This is apparent in Chapter 8, not because of her failure to mix but because of her condescension when she does so. Her soul writhes in subjection to Birkin. Later she revolts. Birkin's presence is compared to a wall which she must break down. Her murderous intention is quickly translated into action, and she all but kills him. Afterwards she sleeps. It is an indication of her possessed state that she does so: she moves from her trance of passion into the aftermath, almost a post-coital reaction.

Birkin's move to the mill is supervised by Hermione. She continues to possess, and here wants to become his provider too in terms of material things. There is something maternal about this interest, almost as if she is conscious of having wounded her own child. She makes one last attempt to put Ursula off Birkin. She shudders with the idea that if Birkin had asked her to be his slave she would have been only too willing. When Birkin appears she pities him, but resents him too. Her ideas on national consciousness are naturally resented by Birkin. This is Hermione's last gamble. She fails here, as she will fail in life, for mind, knowledge and position cannot replace the simple sincerity of communication and instinctual love. She wants to worship, to adore, and to be adored. But she is tense, predatory and drugged with selfhood.

Other characters

Lawrence creates characters with light brush-strokes as well as through detailed psychological investigation. The *Crich* parents are vividly conjured. *Mrs Crich* is an eccentric – unkempt, forced into conformity in the outward sense, but inwardly apart. Lawrence says 'She looked like a woman with a monomania, furtive almost, but heavily proud.' There is no doubt that she is mentally and emotionally deranged. It is enough to embarrass the family and to call forth Gerald's authority (and condescension). Yet she has a keen and intuitive insight, knowing instinctively that Birkin could be the saving of Gerald. She confers with Birkin, loses her way in the conversation, and even as she tells him that Gerald needs a friend she forgets that he is there. Her past is tellingly given in the chapter called 'The Industrial Magnate', where she opposes her husband's 'creeping democracy' and would even set the dogs on some of his petitioners. She treats her husband with withering sarcasm on this count – 'It's your duty to invite all the rats in the world to gnaw at your bones.' She is isolated, fierce, antagonistic by choice and, as the years pass, she never directly opposes his will; inwardly we are told that she was 'unbroken and unimpaired'. She only sat in her room 'like a moping dishevelled hawk, motionless, mindless.' She has been the focus of his sexual desire, and he has withered and wasted her just as Gerald is to waste Gudrun. She has the insight to see into Gerald, advising him to let the dead bury their dead, telling him that he is hysterical and that he will find himself in 'Queer Street' if he isn't careful. Her contemplation of her dead husband, her crooning tone and her invocation forbidding her children to look like that in death, have a frightening intensity of deranged passion.

Her husband is just as convincing, his authority now undermined, taken over by the son who has a different set of values. He is the benevolent industrial magnate – Mr Crich's god is God, not the machine, and he regards his work-force as an extension of his family. The retrospect on his marriage in Chapter 17 is tense with his frustration during the earlier years. Driven nearly mad by the divisions with his wife, he beat his children and then reaped the whirlwind of his wife's own madness. Now near death, his inward pain is like a strong darkness which will overpower him. He does not admit to himself that he is dying, for his repressions and suppressions are buried in some corner of himself. At the same time he has a completely irrational fear of 'his wife, the destroyer'. He is determined to die without letting her break him. This inner assertion of will in fact keeps him going for some time. His love is given to Winifred, and it is an overwhelming and protective love. Everything must be devoted to making her secure when he is gone. Gudrun is therefore a welcome necessity. His love for this child has taken the place of his love for the miners, who are now kept in tight check by Gerald. He smiles, makes conversation with Gudrun – who is conditioned enough to give him the right answers – and generally succumbs to his end. He is eaten away in death. He dies with a question on his lips, querulous and unanswered.

Winifred is recognizably a Crich child. She is neurotic, spoiled, uncanny, loquacious, makes a great fuss over animals, discusses death (her father's, before it occurs) with Gudrun, and displays talent and promise but not much indication of the character to sustain it. She has some traits which are recognizably like her mother's and a capacity for gushing which makes her an unsympathetic child. Like Gerald, though, she seems to be a victim. The rest of the family are only passingly described: one gets a terrible feeling of anonymity about them, almost as if their parents, their upbringing – and perhaps Gerald's domination – have been too much for them.

Cameos of characters like *Mrs Kirk*, with her invariable gossipy confidences, verge on caricature. The *Brangwen parents* are particularly good, though not emotionally documented to the same extent as the Criches. Brangwen, possessive father, grown now apart from his daughters and particularly the one he worshipped – Ursula – is easily provoked by Ursula's behaviour, whether it is bright, unpredictable or rebellious. The age gap, the differences which occur between parents and children, are accurately captured in Brangwen, whether he is on the way to the water-party and feeling socially self-conscious, or whether he is berating Ursula for her independence, or talking to Birkin about his proposal. He is an impassioned man who has grown older, and no longer has a positive point of contact with his daughters. They are socially and morally beyond him.

One other character stands out in *Women in Love*, and this is *Loerke*. He is at Innsbruck with his boyfriend, and is soon attracted to Gudrun, whom he flatters by affecting to think that she is married. He knows that she is Gerald's mistress, and undermines Gudrun's relationship with Gerald by his insidious influence. He is conversationally adept, enjoys acting, mimicry, mocking, teasing, and exerts a strange and compulsive fascination over Gudrun. His triumph is in his miniscule art, the figure of the girl: Lawrence's triumph is in the art of Loerke's miniscule presentation, which is charged with all the potency of evil. He conveys 'mocking, penetrating understanding'; he feels hatred for his 'young love-companion' in the company of Gudrun, and mocks him ruthlessly. Paradoxically, when he has the chance to talk to Gudrun, at first he won't do it. 'He sat hunched up, as if his spirit were bat-like.' His main theory is that 'Art should *interpret* industry as art once interpreted religion.' In the incident with Gerald he shows bravery – he mocks him despite being knocked down. He has admitted that he loves only for convenience. After Gerald's death he is crushed, frustrated, emotionless, barren.

Style

Lawrence's style is like that of no other writer: it is the direct expression of his intense individuality, so that although his novels are recognizably in the mainstream tradition of plot, setting and character in action, they are different in expression. There is a vivid life and vibrancy about them, as if all experience is heightened.

You will notice as you read through *Women in Love* the sharp, crisp similes and metaphors which are one of the main aspects of his style (he was, after all, a considerable poet). Take the first chapter. Gudrun feels the degradation of her return home, the stares to which she is exposed undermining her tolerance. We are told that 'She felt like a beetle toiling in the dust.' That is immediate, the physicality conveyed economically and oppressively. But Gudrun also has a wider perspective, which Lawrence conveys by employing a different kind of image. She watches the people at the wedding and sees each as being 'like a character in a book, or a subject in a picture, or a marionette in a theatre, as finished creation.' The simile brilliantly conveys Lawrence's narrative method, which is to start with distance and then penetrate beneath distance to individuality. Thus the Crich parents, like Birkin and Gerald initially, are exposed to the sisters' outward view: the inward is later revealed, the complexity of human nature in each case is investigated.

In this first chapter, as elsewhere, Lawrence uses images which have a prophetic force. Thus Gudrun's appraisal of Gerald ('His totem is the wolf') anticipates Gerald's predatory seeking her out, though he is himself in the final analysis defeated by her strength and assertion of will. Hermione's feeling when she finds that Birkin is not at the church ('A terrible storm came over her, as if she were drowning') is part of the insistent imagery which reaches forward to the death of Diana Crich. She herself is compared to 'a sudden surf-rush', while the bridegroom's pursuit of her is conveyed through animalistic and sexual imagery ('his supple haunches working like those of a hound that bears down on the quarry'). It is this kind of imagery, together with references to fire, light, electricity, which invests the novel with a peculiar intensity.

Much of Lawrence's language shows his love of nature. In the chapter called 'Mino', for example, Lawrence conveys the compulsion of the stray cat by saying that she moves 'like a blown leaf along the ground'. In the same chapter, in interaction with Birkin, Ursula is shown as 'pressing back her head like a cobra'. This is vivid, natural, menacing, tense. But Lawrence's usage ranges across the commonplace and invests it with a striking force. Whilst Gudrun is paddling she becomes aware that she is being watched by the men, and 'The colour flew in her face like a flag.' Birkin in reaction against Ursula's delay in accepting his proposal goes to Shortlands intent on seeing Gerald, and we are told that 'He was suspended motionless, in an agony of inertia, like a machine that is without power.' The attentive reader will note the irony of this, for Birkin is about to initiate 'the God of the machine', Gerald, into a new form of relationship (Chapter 20, 'Gladiatorial'). Here the image is expressive of Lawrence's detestation of the industrial age which undermines or kills individuality. This image is symbolic, like the superb image which concentrates the sexual passion which Mr Crich feels for his wife Christiana – 'the white flame . . . the flame of her sex, was a white flower of snow to his mind. She was a wonderful white snowflower which he had desired infinitely.' This, and similar, images constantly reoccur, creating a structural cohesion. The image could, for instance, be transferred, without distortion, to Gerald's wasting lust for Gudrun – flame and snow, warmth and life, cold and death. Lawrence is here exploring the effect of contrasting yet composite imagery. The result is to suggest the momentous contrasts of life within the individual, capturing moods of feeling and desire. This is broad yet cunningly particularized natural imagery, but Lawrence can, with sudden transitions, convey the simple reaction through the simple, yet how deft, natural image. Thus when Birkin tells Gerald that he, Gerald, thinks of him as a freak, we read that Gerald's 'face opened suddenly, as if lighted with simplicity, as when a flower opens out of the cunning bud.' This is instinct with recognition, a kind of complementary beauty, typical of Lawrence at his best in the matter of linking nature and man in insightful truth. Read the novel with your eyes and ears alert for pictures and resonances, for Lawrence vivifies all that he sees, touches and hears.

One of Lawrence's major effects is achieved through the use of repetition. What other writers avoid, Lawrence exploits and develops, giving to his prose a rhythmic continuity, an authoritative saturation of statements or reactions, from feelings to the complex movement of sexuality. On the Sunday evening after the death of Diana, Birkin calls at the Brangwens to see Ursula. The latter's reaction afterwards shows the extreme mood of conflict which Birkin's feelings for her have opened up. She believes that she *hates* him, and Lawrence uses the word like a pulse-beat in the blood.

> ... Ursula felt such a poignant hatred of him ... fine hatred ... intensified into a pure dart of hate ... the most poignant and ultimate hatred ... It was like a possession. She felt she was possessed. And for several days she went about possessed by this exquisite force of hatred ... She did not know why she hated him, her hate was quite abstract ... she was so transfigured in white flame of essential hate.
>
> It was not temporal, her hatred, she did not hate him for this or for that ... the hate was so pure and gem-like ... her hatred only intensified itself a few degrees ... She could not escape this transfiguration of hatred that had come upon her.

I have given this at length because it is a convenient way of summarizing the major Laurentian technique. The interested student will pick out other images from this sequence, for Lawrence's style is impregnated by patterns of cross-reference, with emphases and images co-mingled to produce the intensity of presentation. With the intimate emotional and physical exchanges between Birkin and Ursula, Gerald and Gudrun, the repetitive rhythms are climactic, ecstatic, the discoveries and consummations caught by the impressionistic registers of the sexual flow. Any emotional experience is given the force of repetition. See particularly Hermione's trance-like state before she strikes Birkin; or, after this incident, the description of Birkin cummuning with nature, which is itself the major healing influence in this novel. Another example is the scene where Gerald seeks the final consummation, death, in the snow. Even such a simple repetition as Winifrerd's wailing cry of her sister's name is effective, dramatic narrative. Life, experience, love-making, mood – all these *are* continually repeated in human experience – and by employing repetition of sound, rhythm and theme Lawrence has mirrored, or echoed, or touched, the qualities of life itself.

Lawrence's dialogue is exact and true. He has an ear for the voice – one could not, for example, confuse Birkin's speech with Gerald's, or even Gudrun's with Ursula's. Here is Birkin in verbal action:

> 'I want you not to care about yourself, just to be there and not to care about yourself, not to insist – be glad and sure and indifferent.' ('Moony')

(In passing, we should note the superb use of dialect by the minor characters, such as the young couple of the market-place who are helped by Ursula and Birkin.)

This verbal delivery is balanced by the exposure of the consciousness of the main characters with devastating detail, so that at the supreme moments of isolation and communication Birkin and Ursula, Gerald and Gudrun are revealed to us. The twentieth-century novelist's art of characterization consists of the presentation of the outward with a complementary exposure of the inward. James Joyce and Virginia Woolf did not invent the inward: they refined it into a seemingly natural flow of consciousness. Lawrence excels at this form of identification. Note how Hermione's outwardness balances with her intense inwardness. Here is an early outward description – 'she was a woman of the new school, full of intellectuality, and heavy, nerve-worn with consciousness. She was passionately interested in reform, her soul was given up to the public cause . But she was a man's woman, it was the manly world that attracts her.' And here is the inward Hermione:

> What delight, what delight in strength, what delirium of pleasure. She was going to have her consummation of voluptuous ecstasy at last. It was coming! In utmost terror and agony, she knew it was upon her now, in extremity of bliss. ('Breadalby')

You will note the repetition, the rhythm of the sentences, and the fact that the movements of the consciousness are being *described*, in other words, they are not so completely within as, say, in Molly Bloom in James Joyce's *Ulysses*. But what is recognizably twentieth-century is the Freudian sexuality of the extract: death and consummation are one and the same thing here, going beyond the sensuality of the sexual experience. Lawrence does not hesitate to show us the naked core of violence that is within his creatures and ourselves. In this way he is a prophet of twentieth-century life, where the veneers approximate to Hermione's and where the action is so often her action too.

Satire and **irony** are also present in *Women in Love*. The two chapters 'Crème de Menthe' and 'Gudrun in the Pompadour' sufficiently indicate Lawrence's contempt for London Bohemianism, at least of this variety, with its pretentious intellecuality and loose living. Halliday and Minette are an incongruous couple, brought together by this indolent way of life. Part of the satire is directed at the gossipy, subjective, self-conscious conversation, part at the unhealthy sexuality – the sexuality of the promiscuous, the sexuality of the head rather than the heart. There is little doubt that Gudrun's triumph is meant to reflect Lawrence's condemnation of this sterile existence, where drink and words form the basis for relationships and judgements which have no connection with instinctual life. But Lawrence's irony is aimed at more than Bohemianism. Note the ironic treatment of Hermione's gathering at Breadalby, with its name-dropping and snobbery intellectual talk divorced from reality. Hermione herself is presented ironically, as we have seen from previous quotations in this section, while a different – more compassionate – brand of irony embraces the Crich family. Mr Crich is a misguided failure despite good intentions, Mrs Crich's unpleasantness stems from a marriage which has wrecked her physically and mentally. The Crich inheritance is also given ironic treatment – ironic and fatalistic, since physical, moral or mental death seems to be their lot in life. In life we are in death is a Laurentian theme (see below), and 'Water-Party' exemplifies this. Gudrun and Gerald have come to life in relation to each other when they are parted by death. Later Gerald is compelled by his night fears after his father's death to go to Gudrun. This is ironic in the deepest sense: he is willingly making himself a victim, just as he has been a victim in the past.

Themes

Middleton Murry, in his highly charged (and one-sided) view of Lawrence (*D.H. Lawrence: Son of Woman*, 1931) has written about the love-hate struggle in Lawrence during the writing of *Women in Love*. Certainly the novel is tortured and anguished. The major theme is embraced by the term *conflict*. We see this if we refer once more to that first chapter which is so much more than the opening of a novel – it is at once a synopsis and a prophecy. The sisters of its title are in conflict with their background and with themselves. At twenty-five and twenty-six respectively they are unsettled, and their intimacy with the two men who are to change their lives brings out the deep-rooted nature of their divisions. Both resist change; both succumb to it after a conflict of wills. But whereas the Ursula/Birkin conflict is resolved by Birkin giving love (though he wants more), the Gerald/Gudrun conflict is resolved by death. Both the men are in conflict too – with each other in terms of viewpoint, though this gradually resolves itself in the initiatory blood-brotherhood. It is preceded by physical conflict – 'Gladiatorial' – which makes for a kind of loving. Gerald is at conflict with himself, his isolation, his night fears, the mark of Cain forces him to seek assurance or to dominate in work, in family and in love. He experiences conflict over Gudrun, and also over Birkin's initiation to swear an eternal bond between them. Birkin's conflict is with Hermione, with his job, with society and the nature of twentieth-century man, and also with Ursula, who demands love when he wants to go beyond love. Hermione is in awful conflict with Birkin, the head/consciousness/instinct battle being a constant between them. The marriage of the older Criches has always been conflict; the divisions between the two generations of Brangwens are spelled out in every encounter between them. Crich and Gerald are in conflict about the way to treat the men.

Other themes have been indicated in the section on *Style*, but most of them subserve the theme of conflict. The idea of searching beyond love, of making all things possible in sexuality (as in Birkin's licentious mood in Innsbruck), the use of art as symbol, of a friendship beyond friendship between man and man, of seeing nature in all its rich equivalence to man – all these play a part in Lawrence's thematic concerns. The theme of sexuality is of central importance, both Birkin and Gerald in their separate ways trying to deny the pre-eminence of the driving force within themselves.

The exploration of relationships between men and women – and between man and man – is central to the conception of *Women in Love*. Lawrence presents thematic situations – social interaction, for example, whether it be at Breadalby, Shortlands, the Pompadour or the marvellous social party in Innsbruck. A theme may embrace superficial resonances or, more importantly, underline and illustrate the healing power of nature set against the dissonance of modern life.

Settings

The main setting is the Midlands near Nottingham. Here Lawrence grew up, and autobiographical identifications can be made. The important thing is the location within the setting – the significance of Shortlands as a place for social gatherings, and of Breadalby, loosely based on Lady Ottoline Morrell's house at Garsington which was a gathering place for intellectuals patronized by Lady Ottoline during the First World War. The major function of the settings – like those mentioned above and the brief London interludes at the Pompadour and Halliday's flat – are both functional and symbolic. The London ones are indicative of contemporary decadence. The Innsbruck sequence is fascinating – it is both international (in terms of the gathering there) and lyrical and constraining – its isolation speaks differently to different individuals. Birkin, and more particularly Ursula, are moved to new experiences but also to departure. The scenery and the experience of it is either poetic or deadly or both. Location in *Women in Love* subserves the themes which stretch the length of the narrative, for even at the end, after the death of Gerald, Birkin experiences in that lonely place a sense of frustration and conflict that Gerald did not respond fully to his blood-brotherhood overtures. Lawrence has a genius for evoking place and the spirit of place, so that all his settings are imbued with imaginative consciousness. This sense of place gives an immediacy to the characters' experiences.

Structure and plot

The title of the novel in a sense anticipates the form it will take, though it is also about men in love (with women, with man, with something beyond love). There is a balancing treatment of the two sisters, seen together at the beginning, then at Shortlands, both having made their assessments of the two men who are to dominate their lives – in Ursula's case permanently, in Gudrun's temporarily. If Chapter 3 belongs to Ursula, then Chapter 4 is Gudrun's. The balance I mentioned is seen in the following 3 chapters: hitherto we have seen much of Birkin but little of Gerald. Now the balance is redressed – on the train it is Birkin and Gerald, at the Pompadour we concentrate largely on Gerald, and the same applies to Chapter 7 'Totem'. 'Breadalby' (Chapter 8) has the social spread, but is focused sharply on the Birkin-Hermione interaction and aftermath.

There would be little point in continuing to pick out the chapter by chapter sequence, except to say that the plot is furthered by every chapter: even where there is much retrospection, as in 'The Industrial Magnate' (Chapter 17). Note here just how direct the structural control is. The title of the chapter gives, in about equal proportion, the emergence of Gerald as magnate and the decline of his father in the same capacity. The sense of the interaction of time past with time present, as here, is an important constituent of the novel. It is seen elsewhere in the structure, for instance in the interaction of the Brangwen girls with their parents, more potently with the father. It is seen in the tradition of the open-house party which Mr Crich always gives. And so on. The depth at which Lawrence worked, his artistic sureness, is apparent in four other chapters which provide the parallel and constrasting elements in the plot. Chapter 13, 'Mino', has Birkin preaching the need for Ursula's submission to him through the convenient immediacy of the cats' behaviour. In a similar chapter (Chapter 18 'Rabbit'), the focus on the rabbit, Bismarck, is really used to convey to Gerald the essential quality of Gudrun's nature, a significant indicator of their relationship and what will happen to it. It is interesting to note that the chapter 'Gladiatorial' (20) comes between two chapters which point up contrast in a telling way – 'Man to Man' (16) and 'Woman to Woman' (22). The first prepares for the physical, mental and emotional blood-brotherhood encounter. The encounter between Hermione and Ursula, on the other hand, is an extension and contrasting refinement, for Birkin is present, and Hermione's possessiveness and proprietorial taking over of Birkin is seen in her treatment of the cat, even to the extent of excluding Ursula by the simple expedient of talking to it in Italian. Here Lawrence is using a structural variant, contrasting the other animal usages (plus Gerald and the compelling of the mare) with, here, an insidious domestic intimacy calculated to upset Ursula. In other words, though each chapter stands alone as a complete segment of the plot, the interrelationship, the association set up by one chapter with another, gives the novel a running structural coherence. 'Excurse' (Chapter 3) anticipates by association the throwaway 'Exeunt' of the final chapter, with Birkin's meditation on the death of Gerald contrasting with Gudrun's barrenness. 'Death and Love' has a similar central, backwards and forwards effect in the plot. Though its is directly connected with Mr Crich and Gerald's turning towards Gudrun, it looks back to the death of Diana (and the death of love between Mr and Mrs Crich) and forward to the love which leads to the death of Gerald. Lawrence has an artistic awareness which relates everything to everything else, touches the fibres of the reader's associative imagination, sets up chains of connection which make our involvement in *Women in Love* both emotionally and aesthetically pleasing.

General questions

1 Write a character study of Ursula.

Guideline notes

Introduction: refer back to *The Rainbow* briefly, indicate age, job, interests, contrast briefly with Gudrun, say what you glean from the opening chapter. Then develop argument in first paragraph – wondering, dreamy and self-absorbed, focus on Birkin at church, leading to detail on the classroom scene of Chapter 3, reactions to Birkin, Hermione, then frustration.

Reactions and behaviour at Breadalby, then focus sharply on Gerald compelling the mare (contrast briefly with Gudrun), leading to Island, then 'Carpeting' and 'Mino' – Ursula's insecurity, passion, need for love, resentment of Hermione, etc.

From 'Water-Party' to 'Moony' – depression, fear, isolation, capacity for argument, need for love, moods, failure to fully comprehend Birkin BUT her love for him.

Bring out the interaction with Hermione, deepening of relationship with Birkin despite arguments with him and her father, the decision to go away, marriage, the market incident, etc.

Conclusion: final phase, going away, new experiences, effect of travel, rejection of the past, relations with Gudrun – view of Loerke – new (licentious) experiences with Birkin – need to move on – final failure to completely understand Birkin.

2 In what ways do you think that *Women in Love* is a religious novel? Give reasons for your answer.
3 Compare and contrast Ursula and Gudrun, bringing out clearly the differences in their characters.
4 For whom do you feel the most sympathetic interest, Birkin or Gerald? Refer to a number of incidents in your answer.
5 What do you consider to be the most vivid aspects of Lawrence's writing? Quote in support of your views.
6 What impression do you get of Lawrence's views of twentieth-century life in *Women in Love*? Refer closely to the novel in your answer.

7 Write about any *two* of the minor characters in the novel, bringing out the quality of Lawrence's characterization in each case.
8 Show how Lawrence employs the sudden and the violent in *Women in Love* by referring in some detail to any two or three incidents.
9 Write an account of Lawrence's use of *contrast* in this novel.
10 How important are the different settings or locations to our appreciation of *Women in Love*?
11 Summarize as far as you can the nature of Birkin's idealism in the novel, bringing out its various facets.
12 By an examination of any *two* scenes in the novel, indicate Lawrence's ability to create a particular atmosphere.
13 Examine in some detail any conversation – say of three pages or so – and say how true to life you think Lawrence's dialogue is.
14 Examine Lawrence's presentation of any intimate relationship in *Women in Love*.
15 'Sexual fulfilment is the driving force throughout *Women in Love*.' How far would you agree or disagree with this statement?
16 What are the main elements of Lawrence's intensity? Quote in support of your views.
17 Indicate the importance of natural description or imagery in *Women in Love*.
18 Examine the theme of conflict in *Women in Love* with reference to any two characters.
19 'Incomprehensible mysticism.' Would you agree with this assessment of *Women in Love*?
20 Write about any aspect or aspects of *Women in Love* not covered by the questions above.

Further reading

Other novels/stories by D. H. Lawrence

Essential *The Rainbow*

Recommended *Sons and Lovers*
Lady Chatterley's Lover
'Odour of Chrysanthemums', 'The Fox', 'The Prussian Officer', 'The Ladybird', 'The Captain's Doll', 'The Rocking-Horse Winner', etc.

(All the above are available in Penguin Books)

Criticism and Biography There is a D. H. Lawrence industry here, and the reader is advised to steer clear of the sensational as far as possible. The following are recommended:

Graham Hough *The Dark Sun* (Duckworth, 1970)

F. R. Leavis *D. H. Lawrence: Novelist* (Penguin, 1970)

Keith Sagar *The Art of D. H. Lawrence* (Cambridge, 1966)

Laurence Lerner *The Truthtellers: Jane Austen, George Eliot. D. H. Lawrence* (Chatto & Windus)

Harry T. Moore *D. H. Lawrence: The Intelligent Heart* (Penguin)

Harry T. Moore ed. *The Collected Letters of D. H. Lawrence* (Heinemann, 1962)